TABLE OF CONTENTS

Top 20 Test Taking Tips

1. Carefully follow all the test registration procedures
2. Know the test directions, duration, topics, question types, how many questions
3. Setup a flexible study schedule at least 3-4 weeks before test day
4. Study during the time of day you are most alert, relaxed, and stress free
5. Maximize your learning style; visual learner use visual study aids, auditory learner use auditory study aids
6. Focus on your weakest knowledge base
7. Find a study partner to review with and help clarify questions
8. Practice, practice, practice
9. Get a good night's sleep; don't try to cram the night before the test
10. Eat a well balanced meal
11. Know the exact physical location of the testing site; drive the route to the site prior to test day
12. Bring a set of ear plugs; the testing center could be noisy
13. Wear comfortable, loose fitting, layered clothing to the testing center; prepare for it to be either cold or hot during the test
14. Bring at least 2 current forms of ID to the testing center
15. Arrive to the test early; be prepared to wait and be patient
16. Eliminate the obviously wrong answer choices, then guess the first remaining choice
17. Pace yourself; don't rush, but keep working and move on if you get stuck
18. Maintain a positive attitude even if the test is going poorly
19. Keep your first answer unless you are positive it is wrong
20. Check your work, don't make a careless mistake

Basic Human Communication Processes

Chest muscles of respiration

Diaphragm: the large dome-shaped muscle that separates the chest cavity from the abdominal cavity

External intercostal muscles: short muscles located between the ribs

Serratus posterior superior: an upper back muscle originating from the lower neck and attaching to the upper ribs

Levator costarum brevis and longus: back muscles that attach from the sides of each thoracic vertebra to the tips of the ribs. There are twelve on each side.

Chest muscles in inspiration

In the diaphragm, contraction causes the chest to expand drawing air into the lungs.

The external intercostals elevate the rib cage to expand the lungs for inspiration.

The serratus posterior superior elevates the rib cage to expand the lungs for inspiration.

The levator costarum brevis and longus elevate the rib cage to expand the lungs for inspiration

Abdominal muscles of respiration

Latissimus dorsi: large flat triangular muscle originating from the upper arm extending to the lower back

Rectus abdominus: thick muscles covering the front part of the abdomen

Internal oblique abdominus: muscles covering the lateral part of the abdomen

Transverse abdominus: lateral abdominal muscles lying underneath the internal obliques

Quadratus lumborum: muscles arising from the upper pelvic bone attaching to the lower vertebral bones of the back

Abdominal muscles in exhalation

The latissimus dorsi keeps the rear part of the abdomen balanced for exhalation.

The rectus abdominus contract the lower back to assist in expelling air out of the lungs.

The internal oblique abdominus contract the abdominal wall to assist in expelling air from the lungs.

The transverse abdominus contract the abdominal wall to assist in expelling air from the lungs.

The quadratus lumborum contracts the lateral portion of the abdominal wall to assist in exhalation.

Phonation

Phonation is the production of sounds of speech. The structure responsible for sound production is the larynx, otherwise known as the voice box. The larynx is in the lower neck and houses the vocal folds. The larynx lies at the top of the trachea (windpipe) and esophagus. The vocal folds are principally involved in the production of sound. Air is exhaled from the lungs and passes through the larynx. As air passes, the vocal folds vibrate to produce sound. These vocal folds are also important to prevent ingested food from entering the lungs. The amount of forced air that passes through the vocal folds controls the volume of speech sounds. The movement of the vocal folds is controlled by the cranial nerve X, otherwise know as the vagus nerve.

Myeloelastic-aerodynamic theory

Producing sounds requires the rapid cycle of the opening and closing of the vocal folds. As the air leaves the lungs and reaches the vocal folds, air pressure builds and forces the folds apart. This makes the folds vibrate. As air continues to pass through the folds, the increased air speed flowing across the folds forces them to stick together again: this is called the Bernoulli effect. The arytenoid cartilages and associated muscles hold the vocal folds together. The thyroid and cricoid cartilages control tension on the vocal folds and cause changes in voice pitch.

Anatomical structures that are responsible for voice resonance

Resonance is the alteration of sounds produced by the larynx.

The following structures serve to alter sounds:
- Pharynx: located just beyond the throat and nasal cavity. Both air and food pass through this space.
- Nasal cavity: principal in creating /m/ and /n/ sounds
- Velum: soft area in roof of the mouth near the back of the throat that moves back or is lifted in the production of sounds
- Oral cavity: the main resonating source for sounds in English

Mouth structures involved in articulation

Articulation refers to the manner in which the mouth structures move in order to produce speech. The following mouth structures are important for articulation:

Pharynx: divided into three parts:
1. Laryngopharynx, first portion of pharynx beginning just before the larynx terminating at the base of the tongue
2. Oropharynx, beginning at the base of the tongue and terminating at the soft palate
3. Nasopharynx terminates at the level of the nasal cavity

Pharynx: The laryngopharynx and oropharynx give resonance to speech sounds. The nasopharynx gives resonance to the /m/ and /n/ speech sounds.

Soft palate: Elevation of the soft palate during speech causes separation of the mouth from the nasal cavity. If this function is defective, the voice will sound produce a nasal sound.

Hard palate: The contact of the tongue against the hard palate is essential in producing many speech sounds.

Mandible: This bone is responsible for the opening and closing of the mouth.

Teeth: Aside from chewing, the teeth assist in the production of several sounds. For example, the /th/ sound is produced by the tongue against the upper teeth.

Tongue: Aside from eating, the action of the tongue is important in the production of many sounds.

Lips and cheeks: Their movement is important in the production of all sounds.

Cranial nerves involved in speech production

Cranial nerve 5 (V), trigeminal nerve, controls the muscles of the mandible causing movement in every direction and innervates part of the soft palate to open the breathing tube.

Cranial nerve 7 (VII), facial nerve, controls the muscles that lower the mandible and controls the muscles of the lips.
Cranial nerve 10 (X), vagus nerve, controls the movement of the soft palate (velum) and pharynx.

Cranial nerve 11 (XI), spinal accessory nerve, controls the movement of the soft palate (velum) and pharynx.

Cranial nerve 12 (XII), hypoglossal nerve, assists in lowering the mandible and controls all movements of the tongue.

Brain stem

The brain stem is made up of the midbrain (mesencephalon), pons (metencephalon), and medulla (myelencephalon). Cranial nerves V (trigeminal) and VII (facial) arise from the pons thus controlling soft palate, mandible, and lip movements. Cranial nerves X (vagus), XI (accessory), and XII (hypoglossal) arise from the medulla thus controlling soft palate, pharynx, mandible, and tongue movements. The brain stem also integrates with other brain structures to control respiration and alertness. The ability to produce coordinated respiration and levels of consciousness can effect speech production.

Reticular activating system, basal ganglion, and cerebellum

The reticular activating system sits at the core of the brain stem and assists in translating sensory input into motor output. It is also vital in maintaining alertness and consciousness.

The basal ganglion lies deep within the brain and serves as a connection between the frontal lobe of the brain with more complex centers of the brain. This structure is responsible for adapting and directing the mechanical movements of speech that have been initiated in the brain cortex.

The cerebellum is located behind the brain stem and is responsible for the rate of speech.

Cerebrum

Frontal lobe: the front portion of the cerebrum. The major areas of speech are located here. The primary motor cortex controls the voluntary movements of the muscles of speech. The supplemental motor cortex controls speech planning. Broca's area is found only on the left side of the cerebrum and is important in the production of the fine-motor muscle activities involved in speech.

Parietal lobe: the upper side portions of the cerebrum. There are two areas of the parietal lobe important in speech. The supramarginal gyrus integrates sensory inputs allowing oral reading and writing comprehension. The angular gyrus integrates sensory inputs providing reading, writing, and object naming comprehension.

Temporal lobe: the lower sides of the cerebrum. There are two major areas of speech in the temporal lobe. The primary auditory cortex (left side for most) takes verbal communication and processes the sounds into recognized words.

Wernicke's area is responsible for verbal and written language comprehension.

International Phonetic Alphabet (IPA)

The International Phonetic Alphabet (IPA) was developed by linguists to provide a way to standardize the representation of the sounds of spoken language. Through a system of symbols, speech sounds are standardized according to the manner in which they are pronounced. This allows a uniform method for speech and language professionals around the world to assess and describe spoken words with the use of phonetic transcriptions. Phonetic transcriptions are represented by placing phonemes (the smallest units of sound) between slash marks / /. Allophones (spoken variations of phonemes) are placed between brackets [ ]. Diacritical markers are symbols or marks used over a letter to distinguish its sound in different words.

Phonetic alphabet

The letters of the phonetic alphabet are listed along with examples of their pronunciation.

/ɔ/ wall, /b/ back, /d/ dog, /e/ cake, /f/ fat, /g/ good, /h/ hat, /i/ feet, /j/ year, /k/ kiss, /l/ late /m/ mug, /n/ nut, /o/ open, /p/ pull, /r/ ran, /s/ sap, /t/ tone, /u/ loop, /v/ vest, /w/ wind, /z/ zip, /æ/ cap, /ɔ / cough, /ə / about, / ŋ/ fang, /ʌ/ cut, /ɪ/ bit, / ʃ / wish.

/ ʒ / measure, / θ / think, / ð / rather, /e/ men, /ʊ / foot,   / ɝ / hurt, / ɚ / later, /eɪ/ lane, /aɪ/ bike, /oʊ / coat, /aʊ / cow,   /ɔ ɪ/ boil, /IU/ mute, / tʃ / cheap, / dʒ / jump

Distinctive feature approach and the place-voice-manner approach

Distinctive feature approach: a vowel or consonant is characterized according to the presence (+) or absence (–) of a particular feature

Place-voice-manner approach: applies to the classification of consonants based on three phonetic features:
1. Place of articulation: the anatomical location, velum, lips, or tongue, where sounds are initiated. For example, placing the tongue against the back of the upper teeth produces /l/.
2. Voicing: refers to the presence or absences of sounds that are produced via the vibration of the vocal folds. Linguists refer to voiced vs. voiceless sounds; for example, /b/ is a voiced sound while /p/ is voiceless.
3. Manner of articulation: the method of which the vocal cord moves in the production of sounds. For example, the /n/ is produced by air passing from the vocal folds through the nasal cavity.

Dimensions of mouth movement in the production of vowel sounds

Lip position makes sounds either rounded or unrounded. Vowel sounds produced with the lips in a circular position are said to be rounded. Those that are produced with the lips in a relaxed position are said to be unrounded.

Tense vowels are produced with more muscular tension and lax vowels are produced with less.

Tongue height produces vowel sounds that are said to be high, middle, or low with regard to where they are produced in the mouth.

Tongue position forward or retracted produces vowel sound that are said to be front, central, or back with regard to where they are produced in the mouth.

Ways that sounds can change one another

Phonetic adaptation refers to the alteration in the movement of the physiologic vocal structures in the pronunciation of a phoneme due to the preceding phoneme.

Assimilation refers to the alteration of a speech sound because of an adjacent sound. For example, in the phrase paint zone the /z/ is now voiceless because of the preceding voiceless /t/.

Coarticulation refers to both the process of adaptation and assimilation whereby speech sounds vary due to the influence of adjacent sounds. Two different articulators move at the same time to produced two different sounds. For example, examine the variations between the /k/ sounds in the words keep and cool.

Suprasegmental

Suprasegmentals (properties of prosody) are features of speech that give speech added meaning and context. Suprasegmentals can be influenced by gender, emotion, or culture. However, there are several suprasegmentals that are most important in the impact of speech production:

- Length of vowels and consonants
- Syllable stress
- Rate of speech
- Pitch or tonal change of words or sounds
- Volume or loudness of speech
- Juncture, pauses between words; sometimes called vocal punctuation

Frequency and pitch

Sound is a result of vibrations of molecules through air, liquid, gas, or solids. Frequency is one of two important features of vibrations of sound. This is the measurement of the number of cycles of vibratory motion per second (Hz). The properties of the vibrating object affects the frequency; however, the medium (air, liquid, gas, or solid) through which sounds are transmitted does not affect its frequency. However, solids with a higher density, such as metal, will transmit sounds faster than more elastic materials.

Pitch is the change in perceived sound. High frequency sounds are perceived as higher pitch. The human ear can perceive frequencies of 20 Hz to 20,000 Hz but is more responsive to frequencies below 1,000 Hz.

Amplitude and loudness

Along with frequency, amplitude is one of two important features of the vibratory motion of sound. Amplitude refers to the strength of the sound. Another way to characterize amplitude is sound pressure. Higher amplitudes produce more intense sounds. Loudness refers to the perception of sound amplitude. Higher amplitudes are perceived as louder sounds. The units of sound loudness are called decibels (dB). The loudness of normal conversation speech typically is between 50 and 70 dB. Sounds that exceed 100 dB may be damaging to the ear.

Components of language

Phonology: the physical production of voiced sounds

Morphology: the study of the structure of words

Syntax: the manner in which words are brought together to form a meaningful sentence

Semantics: the meaning that is expressed in a word, phrase, or sentence

Pragmatics: the use of words, phrases, or sentences in the correct social context

Morpheme

A morpheme is the smallest grammatical unit of language. It may be a word, prefix, or suffix. It is distinctive from phonemes in that it always has meaning. There are two major categories of morphemes: free and bound. A free morpheme is one that forms a word or can stand alone, like the words cat or pray.

A bound morpheme is a grammatical unit that attaches to words to create other words but cannot form a word alone. An example of a bound morpheme is the prefix dys– that forms the word dysfunction.

Several important varieties of morphemes are the inflectional type that mark plurality or tense, such as the endings –s, –ing, and –ed.

Derivational morphemes are those that produce additional word meanings when placed in front or at the end of words, such as our previous example dys– as in dysfunction and

–ness in the word laziness.

Mean length of utterance

The mean length of utterances (MLU) in morphemes is an important tool in describing children's speech development. The MLU is calculated by dividing the number of morphemes by the number of utterances.

To calculate MLU, choose 100 consecutive utterances and count all morphemes, even if used incorrectly. Do not count repeating words like no, no. Do not count extraneous words like um.

- At ages 1 to 2, children should have an *MLU* of 1.0 to 2.0
- At ages 2 to 3, expected *MLU* 2.0 to 4.0
- At ages 3 to 4, expected *MLU* 3.0 to 5.0
- At ages 4 to 5, expected *MLU* 4.5 to 7.0
- At ages 5 to 6, expected *MLU* 6.0 to 8.0
- At ages 6 to 7, expected *MLU* 6.5 to 8.5
- At ages 7 to 8, expected *MLU* 7.0 to 9.0

Semantics

Vocabulary development: Important aspects of vocabulary development include the number of words used and understood. Also important is the familiarity with opposites, synonyms, homonyms, humor, and symbolic language. This development depends upon the extent of the child's exposures.

The idea of fast mapping refers to the ability of a child to gain knowledge of new words and concepts with a small number of exposures to them.

Word relationships: Children in the early stages of speaking (1 to 2 years) may use overextensions (e.g., uses mama to refer to all women) or underextensions (e.g., only the child's favorite train can be a toy). The ability to categorize words is important in language development.

Pragmatics

Language function: Children should be able to expand the ability to label and describe objects. They must develop conversational skills such as taking turns while speaking, maintaining topical conversation, and being logical. Language context should be coherent and intelligible as they grow older.

Pragmatic skills: There are several important pragmatic skills in language development. These include the ability understand and use indirect speech and the ability to maintain effective discussion (discourse.)

Both language function and pragmatic skills may be influenced by culture.

Semantic relations that young children (12 to 18 months) in the single-word phase (holophrastic stage) should be able to express verbally

Action: Example: Car go

Attribute: Example: Yummy cookie

Denial: refers to a refutation in response to a statement or question. Example: No doggy

Disappearance: Example: Wagon gone

Existence: Example: That car

Locative action: Example: Truck here

Possession: Example: Dolly mine

Recurrence: Example: More juice

Rejection: Example: No milk

Semantic relations that children 18 to 24 months in the two-word phase should be able to express verbally

Action-object: Example: Drive car

Agent-action: Example: Boy sing

Agent-object: Example: Mommy hat (Mommy's hat)

Action-locative: Example: Go park (Let's go to the park.)

Demonstrative-entity: Example: That toy (not this toy, but that toy)

Entity-attributive: Example: Big horse

Entity-locative: Example: Dolly chair (The dolly is on the chair.)

Instrumental (verb and noun): Example: Sweep broom (sweep with the broom)

Notice: Example: Bye kitty

Nomination: Example: That horse (That is a horse.)

Recurrence: Example: More cookie

Developmental milestones of speech and language during the first year of life

Birth to 3 months:
- Vocalizes with cooing sounds
- Tracks voices or faces with eyes
- Reacts to loud noises or pain by turning head or crying
- Smiles in response to stimuli

3 to 6 months:
- Uses various vocalization sounds, which mature into multisyllables
- Recognizes and responds to familiar faces

6 to 12 months:
- Understands a few words or simple commands
- Recognizes own name
- Communicates needs by gesturing to objects
- Attempts to imitate speech

Developmental milestones of speech and language during years 1 and 2

12 to 18 months:
- Follows simple requests
- Requests objects
- Names 5 to 10 objects
- Language mostly consists of nouns
- Begins to express own emotions and experiences
- Begins to initiate conversation
- Uses single words (holophrases) to express objects, needs, and actions

18 to 24 months:
- Uses multiword responses (2 to 3 words)
- Uses verbs and adjectives in combination with nouns
- Can express up to 50 words and understand nearly 200 words by age 24 months
- Can use the personal pronoun, usually *me*

Developmental milestones of speech and language during years 2 through 4

2 to 3 years:
- Starts to use plurals, personal pronouns, and regular past tense verbs; misuses irregular past tense verbs
- Can express about 500 words and understands about 3,500 words
- Can use 3 to 4 word responses and can now ask simple questions
- Can follow two-step requests
- Can state age, name, and some body parts
- Demonstrate some intent in most aspects of communication

3 to 4 years:
- Uses plurals, past tense, prepositions, pronouns, some irregular words, possessives, and conjunctions
- Starts to use and understand complex expressions and questions
- Able to use about 1,000 words and can understand about 4,000 words
- Understands comparative words and opposites
- Most speech comprehensible to others

Developmental milestones of speech and language during years 4 through 8

4 to 5 years:
- Uses complete sentences, future tense, possessive pronouns, and irregular plurals
- Able to use about 6,000 words and can understand about 9,000 words
- Understands simple time concepts
- Begins to define and inquire about words and concepts
- Able to tell stories and jokes
- All speech comprehensible to others

5 to 6 years:
- Uses concepts learned from ages 4 to 5 with fewer grammatical errors
- Understands spatial relationships• Uses superlatives, adverbs, and conjunctions to join complex sentences; understands explicative language

6 to 7 years:
- Has mastered most tense and plural forms and is using *–ing* ending words (gerunds)
- Able to perform simple reading and writing

7 to 8 years:
- Able to converse at nearly adult level
- Able to retell a complex story with appropriate spatial content, social meaning, and figurative expressions

Theories of language acquisition

Nativist theory holds that children have an innate or genetic ability to learn and organize language but need the presence of other people in order to learn language to its full potential.

Behaviorist theory holds that the acquisition of language is similar to any learned behavior. Children are conditioned by positive or negative reinforcement to learn language. Furthermore, a particular language is learned as a product of a particular environment.

The social interactionism theory of language acquisition holds that language is acquired through interaction with the environment. This theory holds that language is learned by the drive to be social.

Cognitive development

Jean Piaget was a Swiss developmental physiologist who was well known for his work in developing his theory of cognitive development. He observed thousands of children and theorized that there were four stages of cognitive development.
1. Sensorimotor stage (birth to 2 years): This stage begins with the development of reflexes, habits, and coordination. Children develop coordination, object permanence, and begin creativity.
2. Preoperational stage (2 to 7 years): Child begins to use mental symbols to represent objects (symbolic functioning). Child can attend only one aspect of a situation (centration) and is egocentric in his thinking.
3. Concrete operations stage (7 to 11 years): Child is able to use logic appropriately.
4. Formal operations stage (after age 11): Child begins to develop the ability to think abstractly.

Information processing theory

The information processing theory is that children learn to think the same way that a computer processes information. Just like a computer, a human takes information, organizes it, stores it, and relates it in order to present it in a logical way by actions, speech, or writing. The theory holds that information gained from previous experience is translated or programmed, and this ability to encode and generalize information is central in problem solving. Once encoded, input is stored in the brain in the form of memory. The important components of memory are sensory units (the part of the brain that receives all the information from the environment), short-term memory (the part of the brain where information is stored temporarily), and long-term memory (the part of the brain where information is held indefinitely). Furthermore, the information processing theory says that humans have a finite capacity for amount and type of information it can handle. The theory further purports that humans, especially children, can learn to improve the efficiency with which they process information and improve their ability to learn. This can be achieved by creating a more receptive learning environment that facilitates increased attention, organization, illustration, and repetition.

Distinctive features concept

In the distinctive features concept, phonemes have unique characteristics that distinguish them. These unique sounds are characterized using a binary system to indicate the presence (+) or absence (–) of the particular sound feature. The important features that represent the major classes of sounds are:

- Consonantal: sounds made by the constriction of the vocal tract. Example: consonantal (+) /g/ in the word gate and the nonconsonantal (–) /h/ in the word hat.
- Sonorant: sounds made without turbulent airflow in the mouth and can be produced continuously at the same pitch. Example: sonorant (+) /m/ in the word make and nonsonorant (–) /d/ in the word dog.

Manner of articulation

Manner of articulation features:
- Nasal: sounds produced with the production of air through the nasal tract, as in the sounds /n/ and /m/.
- Voiced: sounds made by vibrating the vocal tract. Example: voiced (+) /d/ in the word dog and the unvoiced (–) /p/ in the word pet.
- Strident: nonsonorant sounds made with turbulent airflow and are produced using high mouth friction. Example: strident (+) /f/ in the word face and nonstrident (–) /s/ in the word sat.
- Continuant: sounds produced with a continuous stream of air through the vocal tract. Example: continuant (+) /w/ in the word wind and noncontinuant (–) /t/ in the word time.
- Lateral: sounds produced by the elevation of the center of the tongue to the roof of the mouth. Example: lateral (+) /l/ in the word lake and nonlateral (–) /r/ in the word rat.

Place of articulation

Place of articulation features:

- Coronal: sounds produced by using the tip of the tongue in the mouth anteriorly, as in the sound /l/, extended as in /th/, or more posterior as in the sound /d/. An example of a noncoronal sound is /j/ in the word jump.
- Dorsal: sounds produced with the midportion of the tongue in the mouth in the high position, as in the sound /g/, in the low position as in the sound /h/ in the word hang, or back position as in the /k/ as in the word kite. An example of a nondorsal sound is /w/ in the word wind.
- Labial: sounds produced using the lips. Example: labial (+) /b/ in the word ball and nonlabial /h/ in the word hat.

Manner of articulation concepts of the place-manner approach to word sounds and the phonemes that correspond to each category

Stops (plosives) are produced by stopping the airflow through the oral and nasal cavities. Stop phonemes: /b/, /d/, /g/, /k/, /p/, /t/

Nasals are produced by passing air from the vocal tract through the nose. Nasal phonemes: /m/, /n/, /h/

Fricatives are produced by creating friction and forceful air through the vocal tract. Fricative phonemes: /f/, /h/, /s/, /v/, /z/, /t/, /d/, /ʃ/, /ʒ/

Affricatives are phonemes that begin their sound like a stop and releases like a fricative. Affricative phonemes: /tʃ/, /dʒ/

Glides are produced without creating major friction or major obstruction of the vocal tract. They are pronounced by changing the movement of the vocal tract during pronunciation. Also called semivowels or semiconsonants, they always precede vowels. Glide phonemes: /w/, /j/

Liquids are produced with the least amount of friction or obstruction of the vocal tract. Liquid phonemes: /l/, also called a lateral due to release of air on the sides of the tongue; /r/, also called a rhotic because sound is made by placing back of tongue against the alveolar ridge

Place of articulation concepts in the place-manner approach to word sounds and the phonemes in each category

Bilabials are produced by placing the lips together. Bilabial phonemes: /b/, /m/, /p/

Labiodentals are produced by placing the bottom lip against the upper teeth. Labiodental phonemes: /f/, /v/

Linguadentals are produced by the tongue contacting the upper teeth. Linguadental phonemes: /t/, /d/

Lingua-alveolars are produced by the tip of the tongue contacting the alveolar ridge. Lingua-alveolar phonemes: /d/, /l/, /n/, /t/, /s/, /z/

Linguapalatals are produced by the tongue contacting the roof of the mouth. Linguapalatal phonemes: /j/, /r/, / tʃ /, /dʒ /, /ʃ /

Linguavelars are produced by the back of the tongue contacting the velum. Linguavelar phonemes: /k/, /g/, /h/

Glottal sound is produced by passing air through the larynx (vocal folds). Glottal phoneme: /h/

American Speech-Language-Hearing Association (ASHA) guidelines

Speech pathologists must be mindful of cultural differences that may affect the delivery of treatment in certain populations. Many aspects of speech that are found in a particular culture may affect the evaluation and treatment process. Care must be taken not to misinterpret these culturally different communication styles as speech or intellectual deficits. Furthermore, some standardized tests may not be appropriate in the assessment of some clients due to cultural differences. Therefore, it is important that speech pathologists be aware of differences in communication styles that are culturally based. Any multicultural or multilingual information that affects communication should be incorporated in the assessment and treatment plan. Treatment should not be directed toward changing culturally specific speech, but to treat any specific speech or reading disorders that exist. Culturally sensitive testing materials should be used when appropriate.

African American English (AAE)

African American English (AAE) is thought to have its origins in West African tribal languages. During the slave trade, many Africans developed a language of communication among each other and with Americans already living here. This language was further refined in the southern United States. The prevalence of AAE used among African Americans is highly dependent on socialization. Most users can switch between Standard American English and AAE. The ability to speak AAE has no bearing on intellectual ability. The factors that influence the use of AAE are:

- Age: Younger persons use AAE more frequently than older persons do.
- Location: There is more AAE spoken in rural locations than in urban ones. AAE is more prevalent in southern states than in the west.
- Socioeconomic status: AAE is spoken more frequently in those of lower income areas compared to higher income areas.
- Social and peer group: Those persons who have more associations with Standard American English speakers are less likely to use AAE.

Phonemic patterns of African American English

- Diphthongs are reduced to monophthongs. For example, *fly* /flaI/ is pronounced *fla*.
- Consonant clusters at the end of words are reduced. For example, the word *past* is pronounced *pas*.
- •The /th/ sound /ð/ in the beginning of some words is rep laced with /d/, and the / θ ⌐ sound at the end of some words is replaced with /f/, /d/, /t/, or /v/. For example, the word *this* becomes *dis*; the word *booth* becomes *boof*.
- When /r/ sounds are at the end of words, they are dropped unless followed by a vowel. For example, the word *pour* becomes *po*.
- The terminal /l/ sound is often deleted. For example, the word *fool* becomes *foo*.
- When a nasal /n/ or /m/ sound follows a vowel, the nasal consonant is sometimes deleted and the vowel is nasalized. For example, the word *man* becomes *mã*.

- When the vowels *i* and *e* come before a nasal sound, they are both pronounced /I/. For example, the words *thin* and *then* are pronounced the same.

Grammatical patterns of African American English

- The verb *to be* is either omitted in sentences or used differently to mark aspect in verb phrases (deletion of copulas). For example, *She cookin'* = She *is cooking*. *She be cookin'* = She *is always cooking*.
- The reversal in order of phonemes containing s-clusters. For example, the word *ask* becomes *aks*, and the word *grasp* becomes *graps*.
- The words *ain't* and *can't* are use to produce negative sentences. For example, *She ain't had no books* = *She had no books*. *Can't nobody tell him nothin'* = *No one can tell him anything*.
- Contractions are dropped and the simple pronoun is used. For example, *Where your hat?* = *Where's your hat?*
- There is a lack of subject verb agreement. For example, *Mary walk to the store.* = *Mary walks to the store.*

Phonemic patterns of Spanish-influenced English

- The substitution of /ch/ for /sh/; for example, the word *ship* is pronounced *chip*.
- The substitution of /b/ for /v/; for example, the word *vote* is pronounced *bote*.
- The sound /th/ becames /d/, /t/, or /z/; for example. the word *thing* becomes *ting*.

- The sound /j/ becomes /y/; for example, the word *jump* becomes *yump*.
- The sound /I/ is pronounced /i/; for example, the word *fit* becomes *feet*.
- The omission of /h/ at the beginning of words; for example, *huge* becomes *uge*.
- The substitution of /θ/ for /s/; for example, *estranged* becomes *ethranged*. This is exclusively found in speakers from Spain.
- The terminal /s/ is deleted in many words in the Caribbean Spanish accent.

Accent modification

An accent is the particular pronunciation of English words based on the country of origin or particular region of the United States. Some persons may want to reduce their accent to improve other's comprehension or to obtain a particular job requiring a high level of Standard English pronunciation. Those persons wishing to reduce their accent will call on a speech pathologist. Although an accent is not considered a speech disorder, there are important aspects of training Standard English. There is typically no reimbursement on state or private health plans for this service. Accent modification is not a part of any school service. Therefore, it is usually a private pay therapy. Accent modification begins with a full assessment of pronunciation patterns. Training is directed toward mouth position, intonation, and speech rhythm training.

Basic interpersonal communication skills (BICS) and cognitive-academic language proficiency (CALP)

Children who acquire two languages simultaneously from infancy (simultaneous bilingual acquisition) tend to learn both languages with minimal difficulty. However, when a second language is introduced before the complete proficiency of the first language is gained, there is typically a decrease in deficiency of both languages for a time. Those children who immigrate into the United States speaking a different language may take an average of 2 years to develop a proficiency in spoken English if there is normal exposure to the language. However, these children may take 5 years to develop a level of academic proficiency in English. This gap between basic interpersonal communication skills and cognitive-academic language proficiency is an important realization when educating English-as-second-language students. These children are at risk of being labeled as having communication or speech disorders.

Individuals with Disabilities Education Act (IDEA)

The Individuals with Disabilities Education Act mandates educational services and provides rights to children with a range of physical, cognitive, and emotional disabilities. Among those protected are children with speech, communication, or learning disabilities. Individual states may also allow for certain circumstances in which children need special education. Certain children who are culturally and linguistically diverse and in need of speech therapy come under the protection of the IDEA. The IDEA mandates the following:

- Materials used in evaluations must be selected and delivered in a way that is not racially discriminatory or culturally biased.
- Evaluations must be made available in the language most efficiently used by the client.
- English deficiency is not a sole determining factor of a child's

- 17 -

qualification for the term *disabled*. Therefore, testing must be directed at evaluating the specific disability rather than for English proficiency.

- Multicultural education should be available as needed for those clients with speech disorders.

Assessment of culturally and linguistically diverse clients

- Speech pathologists should exercise caution when using standardized tests for evaluations. Care must be taken to ensure that the tests do not hold bias for particular clients, which may inhibit an adequate assessment. Standardized tests translated into alternative languages are not recommended. Tests developed particularly for certain populations are more relevant.
- Dynamic assessment using the classroom and natural environment is an alternative to standardized tests.
- The use of an interpreter is acceptable; however, this method should be administered wisely. Choose a qualified interpreter with the caregiver's permission when a minor or legally conserved person is involved. Make sure that the interpreter has a clear understanding of all objectives and is aware of the client's background and needs.
- Speech therapy in the client's native language is an acceptable practice when appropriate. Therapy should be directed at the speech therapeutic objectives rather than correcting grammatical errors.

Innateness, motherese, functional core, semantic features, and critical age hypotheses

Innateness hypothesis: Humans are born with an innate universal grammar.

Motherese hypothesis: The acquisition of language is dependent upon the language of the caretaker.

Functional core hypothesis: Children develop language by defining objects by their functional quality and then by applying conceptual features later.

Semantic features hypothesis: Children acquire a body of basic universal features that define objects. These features expand and become more sophisticated over time.

Critical age theory: The critical period of language acquisition begins at age 2 and ends at age 12. This theory has been largely refuted.

Sequential memory

Sequential memory is the ability to remember details in a particular order. Many children have poor sequential memory, especially those with dyslexia.

Visual sequential memory is required to recall letters, words, and numbers. Poor visual sequential memory causes reading, writing, spelling, and enumeration difficulties. Young children have difficulty learning the alphabet, shapes, and numbers. Many have difficulty with recall of subjects presented to them visually. They often misspell, miscopy, and rearrange letters, words, and numbers. They have difficulty with relating a story in a logical order.

Auditory sequential memory deficits may also be present, which cause sequence

errors when verbalizing long words and
sentences.

Phonological and Language Disorders

Specific language impairment (SLI)

Specific Language impairment (SLI) is a developmental communication disorder that is a pure language impairment. Children with this disorder have normal physical and intellectual development. Their language delay cannot be attributed to any physical cause of developmental abnormality, such as brain injury or autism. These children have impaired expressive and receptive language skills.

Specific features include:
- Failure to use or correctly apply plurality, possessive words, articles, past tense, comparative words, and irregular words
- Inability to form or understand long/complex sentences
- Inability to initiate or maintain age-appropriate conversation

Mental retardation and autism

Mental retardation refers to an impairment of intellectual functioning (IQ <70) due to genetic defects or injuries during gestation or at birth. Mentally retarded children have significant delays in all of the components of language. Although grammatical development occurs in a normal sequence, the language of children with mental retardation usually lacks variety and complexity. It is typical for children to have language that is concrete and repetitive.

Autism spectrum disorder refers to an impairment of social and communication skills. Autistic children may have low, average, or superior intelligence. They often engage in repetitive behavior activities. The language problems with autism run the gamut from severely delay in words, content, structure, and grammar to the inability to make meaningful sentences, despite a large vocabulary. They are unable to interact with others and often do not respond to their names. When they do speak, they may not make good eye contact. Repeating words or phrases (echolalia) is very common.

Asperger's syndrome

Asperger's syndrome refers to a subset of children on the autism spectrum scale. This disorder affects mostly males. These children have deficits in social interactions.

Their repetitive behaviors are similar to other children with autism; however, their language and intellectual abilities are at the higher end of the spectrum scale. Given social interaction problems, language issues are primarily due to poor pragmatics. Therefore, improving the social context of language is the training goal when working with these children. Given the propensity to engage in repetitive behaviors, these children must learn to reduce or eliminate perseverant language.

Brain injuries that affect speech and language in children

Traumatic brain injury results from a blow or a penetrating trauma to the head. Physical trauma may cause transient or long-term deficits in speech comprehension, speech fluency, speech pragmatics, and memory. The most common forms of traumatic brain injury are caused by motor vehicle accidents, falls, sports injuries, firearms, and physical abuse.

Cerebral palsy is a group of early childhood, nonprogressive disorders that cause neurological and motor abnormalities. This disorder is caused by brain injury during pregnancy (e.g., infection, trauma), during delivery (e.g., low oxygen, premature delivery), or just after delivery (e.g., infection, trauma). Children with cerebral palsy typically have movement disorders, such as paralysis, spasticity, seizures, or ataxia (imbalance), or hearing deficits. Language development may range from normal to severe speech articulation abnormalities (dysarthria).

Poverty

Although poverty does not directly cause learning disorders, it can be a contributing factor in many ways. Some low-income families have limited access to health care. Children who have poor health may have difficulty learning. Mothers without prenatal care may have low birth weight children that can go on to learning difficulties. Furthermore, some children born into poverty have a low level of academic and social stimuli at home, which hampers their ability to learn language. Many of these children have delayed speech, poor development of vocabulary, and reading difficulties.

Parental drug and alcohol abuse

Many children from households where parents abuse alcohol or drugs may suffer from neglect or emotional or physical abuse. These children are most likely to develop expressive language delays.

Fetal alcohol syndrome refers to physical and cognitive disorders that occur in children whose mothers used excessive amounts of alcohol during pregnancy. Children with this disorder may have low birth weight, facial abnormalities, and small head circumference. They may have profound cognitive, neurological, and motor developmental delay. They also

may have organ development abnormalities.

Speech and language problems seen in drug and alcohol exposure are gross and fine motor delay; poor eye contact; emotional lability or depression; poor social interactions; lack of attention; poor memory and poor articulation, vocabulary, and communication in general.

Attention deficit hyperactivity disorder (ADHD)

Children with attention deficit hyperactivity disorder (ADHD) have problems with inattention, hyperactivity, or impulsivity, or all three. It is typically diagnosed during the preschool or early elementary school period, given that typical children may not have mastered attention skills before this period. Language problems that may be associated with ADHD are:

- Difficulty processing auditory stimulation
- Difficulty following instructions
- Reading and writing difficulties
- Poor expressive language
- Difficulty in engaging in normal conversational discourse
- Poor social interactions

Phonological processes

The term phonologic processes refer to the manner in which children pronounce speech sounds. Phonological processes can also be referred to as speech errors made by children.

The three major categories are:

- Substitution: The child substitutes one class of speech sounds for another. For example, the child may pronounce the word rat as *wat.
- Assimilation: The child pronounces phonemes similarly

to a nearby phoneme. For example, the word cat is pronounced tat.

- Syllable structure processes: The child alters an entire syllable by deletion or alteration of its sound. For example, the word potato is pronounced tato.

Substitution phonological processes

Affrication: An affricative is substituted for a fricative or a stop. For example, the word cheek becomes teek.

Backing: A posterior pronounced phoneme is replaced by an anterior one. For example, peach is pronounced peat.

Deaffrication: A fricative is substituted for an affricative. For example, the word catch is pronounced cash.

Depalatization: An alveolar fricative or affricative is substituted for a palatal fricative or affricative. For example, the word fish becomes fis.

Gliding: The phonemes /l/ and /r/ are replaced with /j/ and /w/. For example, the word below becomes beyow and the word run becomes wun.

Stopping: A fricative or an affricative is substituted by a stop. For example, the word zipper becomes dipper.

Velar fronting: An alveolar or dental placed consonant is substituted by a velar consonant. For example, the word coat becomes toat.

Vocalization: A vowel is substituted for a consonant. This most commonly occurs in words containing an /l/ or /r/ such that these consonants are replaced with the sounds /o/ or /u/. For example, father is pronounced fatho, and bottle is pronounced bato.

Assimilation phonological processes

Progressive assimilation: a change in the pronunciation of a phoneme because of the effects of a proceeding phoneme. For example, the word zip becomes dip.

Reduplication: duplication of a syllable. For example, the word water becomes wawa.

Regressive assimilation: a change in the pronunciation of a phoneme because of the effects of a preceding phoneme. For example, the word pass becomes pat.

Voicing assimilation: a phoneme is either voiced or devoiced incorrectly. For example, the word card becomes cart, and the word pig becomes big.

Syllable structure processes

Consonant-cluster reduction: A consonant is deleted from a syllable containing adjacent consonants. For example, the word play becomes pay.

Metathesis: Sounds in a word are reversed. For example, spaghetti becomes pisgetti.

Epenthesis: An /a/ or schwa sound is added to a word. For example, black becomes balack.

Diminutization: An /i/ sound is added to the end of a word. For example, the word doll becomes dolly.

Weak (unstressed) syllable deletion: The unstressed syllable of a word is deleted. For example, the word wagon becomes wag.

Final consonant deletion: The final consonant in a word is omitted. For example, the word hat becomes ha.

Articulation errors

Articulation errors occur in children due to some physical inability to produce the correct sound. Thus the child has neurological or motor deficiencies that cause articulation errors. The major physical disorders that may lead to articulation problems are:

- Structural abnormalities of the facial and oral anatomy
- Poor oral-motor coordination
- Hearing loss
- Orofacial myofunctional disorders: abnormality in tongue position at rest and/or when swallowing. The tongue protrudes forward on or past the teeth.
- Dysarthria: a speech-motor disorder due to a neurological injury such as trauma, cerebral palsy, or tumors
- Apraxia: difficulty initiating speech due to deficits in motor planning

Types of articulation errors

Devoicing: the limit or absence of vocal cord vibration to produce sounds. For example, the word pad becomes pat.

Labialization: production of phonemes using excessive lip rounding. For example, the word grow becomes gwow.

Lisp: the production of /s/ or /z/ sounds with tongue touching or protruding through the front teeth (frontal lisp) or with air escaping over sides of the tongue (lateral lisp)

Nasalization: sounds produced by allowing air to escape through the nose

Omissions: deletion of phonemes of words. Ex. hat becomes ha.

Pharyngeal fricative: production of fricatives by using the pharynx
Position error: mispronunciation of phonemes in the initial, middle, or final position of a word

Substitution: the exchange of one class of speech sounds for another. For example, the child may pronounce the word rat as wat.

Stridency deletion: the substitution or deletion of one sound for another. For example, hair becomes air, or chew becomes tew.

Unaspirated: sounds that are normally produced with aspiration (e.g. /p/, /k/, /t/) are pronounced without a strong release of air though the mouth

Vocalic error: mispronunciation of consonants in initial (prevocalic), middle (intervocalic), and terminal syllables (postvocalic)

Abnormalities of the facial and oral anatomy

Ankyloglossia (also known as tongue tie) is a congenital anomaly causing limited mobility of the tip of the tongue. This is due to a short and thick frenulum, which attaches the bottom of the tongue to the floor of the mouth. In infants, this condition may effect feeding due to difficulty swallowing and sucking. Later, speech may be affected. However, not all children with ankyloglossia will have articulation deficits. A v-shaped notch at the tip of the tongue, decreased tongue mobility, and tongue protrusion can identify children with this anomaly. Some children will have difficulty producing the lingual phonemes, such as /t/, /d/, /z/,

/s/, /θ/, /ð/, /n/, /l/. There is controversy whether surgical repair of this condition is necessary.

Oral malocclusions may cause articulation errors. Malocclusions are the misalignment of the upper dental arch (maxilla) and the lower dental arch (mandible). It may also refer to the misalignment of individual teeth. Malocclusions may be inherited, as those seen in tooth overcrowding or large spaces between teeth. Accidents and thumb sucking may also be a cause of malocclusions.

Irwin and Weston's paired-stimuli approach

Irwin and Weston's paired-stimuli approach utilizes words already in the child's vocabulary. An articulation error sound is targeted. Four key words are created, two with the target sound in the initial position and two with the targeted sound in the final position. Ten pictures that suggest words with the targeted sound are selected corresponding to each key word. The key words are arranged around the target word, and the child says the key word, the target word, and the key word again (training string).

The child must master the pronunciation 9 out of 10 times without reinforcement before moving to the next sound.

Cognitive-linguistic approach to articulation-phonological therapy

Cognitive-linguistic approach: This procedure focuses on the pattern of sounds rather than on the treatment of individual sounds.

Distinctive-features approach: Through language sampling, an omitted distinctive feature is identified and that feature is trained with the expectation that it will be generalized among like phonemes.

Minimal-pair-contrast approach: A minimal pair is a set of words that differs by a single phoneme, and that single phoneme conveys a totally different meaning. This approach uses contrasts of features in phonemes (e.g., bilabial consonants, alveolar lingual consonants) of paired words to teach the distinctions in the sounds. The sound used in error is paired with a corresponding substitute. The child will presumably generalize the correct sound to other words containing phonemes of the same feature.

Treatment of phonologic disorders that use the cognitive-linguistic approach

The phonological-knowledge approach is used to treat phonological deficits in children. In this form of therapy, the child's phonological inventory of sounds is assessed. Treatment is directed toward those sounds that are most mispronounced and then progresses to those that are mastered. The child's knowledge of phonological rules is thus expanded.

The phonological-process approach (Hodson and Paden's cycles approach) is used for children with many misarticulated sounds and whose language is very difficult to understand. The child's various phonological processes (errors) are assessed and targeted for treatment. Therapy runs in a cycle of 5 to 16 weekly sessions. A phonological error pattern is treated in one therapy session, and all are addressed within one treatment cycle. In each session, target words are reviewed, and new ones are practiced.

Metaphon therapy

Metaphon therapy is based on children's phonological awareness and capacity to control the structure of language. This therapy is best used with preschoolers with moderate to severe phonological disorders. The approach relies on the assumption that phonological errors are due to incorrect acquisition of the rules of phonology as opposed to difficulty in the motor production of sounds. Furthermore, real-life materials are used as analogies for speech sounds.

Neurological causes of phonation disorders

Paralysis of the vocal folds can be caused by trauma, tumors, strokes, and nerve injury. This may lead to changes in voice volume and pitch. Therapy is aimed at increasing volume and pitch, improving breath control, and optimizing neck and head positioning.

Sposmodic dysphonia are involuntary movements of the muscles of the larynx causing voice breaking and difficulty saying words. Brain stem dysfunction is thought to be the cause of this voice disorder. Botox injections, vocal cord relaxation techniques, medications, surgical widening of the glottis, and recurrent laryngeal nerve resections are among the possible treatments.

Neurological diseases, such as multiple sclerosis, myasthenia gravis, ALS, and Parkinson's disease, may cause vocal cord dysfunction.

Paradoxical vocal fold motion (vocal cord dysfunction) is an episodic abnormal closure of the vocal folds while talking or breathing. Persons with this disorder may wheeze and have hoarseness or difficulty breathing and behave like that of an asthmatic. Local irritants, exercise, acid reflux, coughing, shouting, and stress can trigger spasms. Therapies are aimed at instruction in relaxation of the vocal mechanism.

Scaffolding

Scaffolding refers to the modification or simplification of language to match the student or client. This type of technique is very useful when teaching students a second language. The instructor simplifies language to the level of the student by shortening sentences, using present tense, and avoiding abstract language. The use of visual aids and sentence and paragraph completion prompts are useful in scaffolding language instruction. Exercises that require some hands-on activities are very effective to facilitate learning. When the student becomes more efficient in the language, the scaffold techniques are gradually decreased and then stopped. It is important to involve caregivers and other members of the student's speech and language team before starting this technique.

Speech Disorders

Stuttering

It is estimated that 1% of persons in the United States have stuttered. The usual age of onset is 2 to 6 years old. Boys are 3 times as likely to stutter than girls are. The onset of stuttering after the adolescent years is extremely rare. An estimated 60% of those who stutter recover spontaneously without treatment. However, older children and adults may start stuttering again after an initial recovery. Stuttering tends to run in families, and the familial incidence is higher if there is a female in the family who stutters. Individuals with developmental disorders and neurological impairments have a higher incidence of stuttering. A lower incidence of stuttering is seen in hearing-impaired individuals.

Persons who stutter and their family members are not likely to have a psychiatric or personality disorder.

Stuttering is a disorder in the fluency of speech. Stuttering is diagnosed when:

- The dysfluency rate of all types of dysfluencies of spoken words exceeds 5%
- The frequency of part-word repetitions, speech sound prolongations, and broken words occurs more than in 2% of speech
- The duration of dysfluencies is more than 1 second
- The presence of associated motor behaviors, such as excessive tensing of the facial muscles, mouth tremors, grimacing, rapid blinking, hand wringing, foot stomping, or foot tapping
- Associated breathing abnormalities, such as poor breath control during speaking and abnormal breath holding
- The presence of negative emotions and avoidance behaviors: Many persons who stutter will develop a behavior to disguise or avoid stuttering. They may completely avoid certain situations, such as public speaking. They may substitute words or avoid situations in which certain words have to be used. The prospect of stuttering may produce anxiety, hostility, depression, or passive behaviors.

Dysfluencies that make up the core behaviors of stuttering

Broken words: placing unusually long pauses between words (I want to play with mom– {pause} –my.)

Incomplete sentences: production of incomplete phrases (I want to play. . . I want to . . My mommy will play with me.)

Interjections: placement of sounds, words, or phrases extraneously into speech (I want, um, to play with mommy.)

Pauses: placing unusually long gaps of silence or nonverbal gaps within sentences or phrases (I want {pause} to play with mommy.)

Repetitions: saying a word, part of a word, or a phrase more than once (I wa-wa-wa want to play with mommy.)

Revisions: changing a wording of a sentence, which does not alter the sentences meaning (I want to play: I will throw ball with mommy.)

Sound prolongation: pronouncing a sound for an unusually long duration (I want to play with mmmmmommy.)

Silent prolongation: holding the articulation position of a sound without vocal production

Stuttering is more likely to occur with consonants, the first sound or syllables of words, or the first word of a sentence or clause. Stuttering is most likely to occur with long, complex sentences. Words that are used less frequently are more likely to induce stuttering. Preschool children more often stutter on function words (e.g., conjunctions, pronouns) than content words (e.g., verbs, nouns). Older children and adults stutter more often on content words. Preschool children who stutter are more likely to produce whole-word repetitions than adolescents or adults are.

Stuttering and strong environmental controls

1. The frequency of stuttering can be reduced by repeated oral readings of printed material. This effect, called adaptation, is not sustained. If given the same material in another setting, stuttering will again occur.
2. Most persons will stutter on the same word or position of a sound when repeating oral readings. This effect is called consistency and tends to be a sustained phenomenon. This effect will be repeated among different trials.
3. Words pronounced correctly can be made to stutter. By blocking out the stuttered word of an oral reading, the adjacent word is then stuttered. This phenomenon is called adjacency.
4. The larger the audience, the more stuttering occurs.

Causes of stuttering

Genetic theory: Given that stuttering has a high familial prevalence, some researchers believe that it is genetically driven. However, given the rates of occurrences, a single-gene theory cannot yet be supported with clinical evidence.

Neurological theories: Some researchers believe that stuttering is due to a dysfunction of laryngeal muscle activity, an abnormality of the speech centers of the brain, a brain auditory processing disorder, or a dysfunction in the auditory feedback mechanism of the brain.

Learning and conditioning theory: Studies suggest that stuttering may be a product of certain environmental factors, such as: avoidance behavior, overwhelming speech expectations, or learned behaviors.

Psychosocial theory: In this theory, stuttering is thought to be a psychological disorder or neurosis, like anxiety and depression, whereby the child is undergoing a subconscious psychological conflict.

Stuttering treatment

The assessment of stuttering should include interviews with clients, caregivers, and teachers to develop a case history. Pay attention to caregiver/teacher speech interactions.

Determine the frequency, types, and variability of dysfluencies. Identify any associated motor behaviors, negative emotions, or avoidance behaviors. The Behavior Assessment Battery can be helpful in determining any negative emotional behaviors.

Treatment of stuttering employs either direct or indirect techniques. Indirect treatment involves the modification of the subject's environment, not the direct modification of speech. This is typically done by instructing parents to speak slowly and relaxed when addressing a stuttering child. Theoretically, the child will learn to modify his speech by passive listening. This technique is not effective in more severe stuttering and in older children and adults. In fact, this technique has not been favored by a consensus of speech experts in its effectiveness for even mild stuttering children. Direct treatment involves intentional alteration of speech patterns.

Stuttering modification therapy

Stuttering modification therapy: The goal with this type of therapy is not to eliminate stuttering but to reduce its frequency, avoidance behaviors, and negative emotions associated with it. This therapy encompasses four stages:
1. Identification: The subject learns to identify the characteristics of his stuttering and the behaviors and emotions connected with it in various situations.
2. Desensitization: The subject discloses that he stutters and is made to voluntarily stutter in various situations.
3. Modification: The subject is directed to use easier and more fluent stuttering. This is achieved by using cancellations (stopping after a stuttered word, pausing, and saying the word again); pull outs (stopping in midstutter, pausing, and saying the word slowly with deliberate articulation); and preparatory sets (anticipating difficult words and using more fluent stuttering).
4. Stabilization: The subject uses the first three stages of the therapy and applies them to all situations.

Fluency shaping, fluency reinforcement, and altered auditory feedback therapies

Fluency shaping therapy: This therapy focuses on production of normal fluent speech as opposed to more fluent stuttering as in stuttering modification therapy. Teaching airflow management and speech rate reduction through syllable prolongation achieves this. Once this is mastered, the subject is trained in normal speech emotional intonation (prosody) and speech rate.

Fluency reinforcement therapy: Typically used in young children, this form of therapy models slow, relaxed, and fluent speech. Through the use of pictures and play items, children are rewarded for using fluent speech.

Altered auditory feedback: Delayed auditory feedback devices delay the subjects voice to their ears by a fraction of a second. Masking auditory feedback devices produce sounds that fool the subject into thinking the vocal folds are vibrating. These techniques are very effective in reducing stuttering. However, delayed auditory feedback appears to be more effective in producing more sustained results than masking auditory feedback is.

Cluttering

Cluttering is a fluency disorder caused by disorganized language. Speech is difficult to understand because of abnormalities of speech rhythm, rapid rate of speech, large number of dysfluencies, production of spoonerisms, disorganized thought processes, and lack of awareness of speech deficits. Reading and writing disabilities are common. There is no abnormality in the mechanism of articulation, but rather in the organization of thoughts. Although the exact cause is unclear, genetic factors and brain dysfunctions are being studied. Treatment is difficult because the subjects have little awareness, but typically focuses on reducing the rate of speech and speech planning. Treatment directed at increasing the subject's awareness of abnormal speech are employed and may include the use of auditory devices.

Disorders of voice resonance

Hypernasality refers to sounds produced with excessive nasal quality due to a dysfunction of the velopharyngeal mechanism. Air escapes through the nasal passages because of incomplete closure at the nasopharyngeal junction. The most common causes of Hypernasality is a cleft palate, velopharyngeal insufficiency due to decreased mass or weakness of the muscles of the velum (children who have had tonsillectomies may have decreased muscle functioning of the velum), and functional causes like bad habits or deafness.

Hyponasality refers to the absence of nasal sounds when appropriate. The /m/, /n/, and /ng/ sounds are pronounced incorrectly due to the absence of air leaving the nose during speech. The appropriate nasal sounds are often substituted with /b/, /d/, and /g/ sounds. Hyponasality is typically caused by nasal or nasopharyngeal obstruction due to deviated septum, severe nasal congestion, nasal polyps, or enlarged adenoids.

Phonation disorders resulting from vocal abuse and misuse

Vocal nodules: small, benign growths that develop due to repeated pressure on the vocal folds. These nodules are frequently found in singers. Vocal rest will usually resolve them, and persistence may require surgical intervention.

Granuloma: benign growth that develops typically at the back of the vocal fold. Although the most frequent cause is vocal strain, it can also develop from tracheal instrumentation. These growths cause hoarseness, breathy voice, and constant coughing or clearing of the throat.

Vocal polyps: soft, pedunculated masses that develop on the vocal folds. They can form from medical conditions such as hypothyroidism as well as vocal strain. Vocal rest is the treatment of choice.

Laryngitis: inflammation of the larynx due to vocal cord strain or infections. Vocal rest and alteration of the behaviors causing strain on the folds is the treatment of choice.

Contact ulcers: caused by the forceful closing of the vocal folds. These painful ulcers may also be due to tracheal instrumentation and acid reflux. The offending phonation error can be corrected with speech therapy.

Vocal folds growths that cause phonation disorders

Hemangioma: blood-filled growth in the posterior vocal area typically caused by instrumentation or acid reflux

Leukoplakia: benign, precancerous growth on the surface of vocal structures caused by vocal overuse or irritating substances such as tobacco and alcohol. They appear as white patches in the mouth or anterior vocal folds.

Hyperkaratosis: fleshy growths that occur in the vocal folds considered precancerous. Irritants such as tobacco, alcohol, acid reflux, and vocal strain can be the cause.

Laryngeomalacia: abnormal development of the larynx leading to a floppy cartilage in the epiglottis. This causes turbulent air through the epiglottis producing a rough voice sound. This condition usually requires no treatment, as most children resolve spontaneously by age 3.

Laryngeal papilloma: vocal cord warts caused by the human papilloma virus (HPV). They primarily occur in children and resolve spontaneously around pubescence.

Laryngeal web: a membrane over the glottis. This typically forms due to the consequence of tracheal instrumentation, infection, or injury.

Laryngeal tumors: Both benign and cancerous can cause phonation disorders.

Laryngectomy

Laryngeal cancer is the most common reason for the surgical removal of the voice box. Without vocal cord vibration, the production of well-articulated sounds is very difficult. There are a number of modalities used to restore phonation. External devices are used to produce sounds. The most common external device is the artificial larynx. This is a hand-held apparatus that is pressed against the neck and produces articulated sounds.

Esophageal speech is a method that uses the resonation of the esophagus to produce sounds. Patients recovering from laryngectomies are taught to produce sounds by passing air through the mouth via a method similar to burping or belching. Several words can be produced at a time.

The surgical implantation of speech devices is also done. The most common procedure is the Blom-Singer tracheophageal puncture (TEP). A device is inserted between the trachea and esophagus. When occluded by the patient's finger, the esophagus resonates to produce sounds.

Craniofacial anomalies

Craniofacial anomalies are a group of disorders characterized by the abnormal development of skull and facial bones. These anomalies are most likely caused by genetic defects. The two most common craniofacial anomalies are cleft lip and cleft palate. In these abnormalities, either the top lip or palate does not close completely. There are various levels of severity. Although this abnormality can be surgically treated, children may have significant speech articulation, phonation, and resonance problems. Children with clefts are susceptible to ear infections that may lead to hearing loss and thus causing speech delays. Treatment of resonance disorders when there is an incomplete velopharyngeal closure is difficult and should be considered after surgical intervention. Treatment of clefts should be a part of a multidisciplinary approach with clinicians, caregivers, and teachers.

Craniosynostosis

Craniosynostosis is the abnormal premature fusing of the bones of the skull. This leads to developmental abnormalities of the head and face bones. Genetic defects cause this anomaly. Children with this abnormality typically have a flat midfacial structure and protruding eyes. The most common disorders associated with craniosynostosis are Apert syndrome and Crouzon syndrome.

Apert syndrome is characterized by a sunken midface, webbed feet and hands, occasional hearing loss, and possible cleft palate with hyponasality.

Crouzon syndrome is characterized by widely spaced eyes, underdevelopment of the maxillary area and jaw, and possible cleft palate. These children typically have hearing loss and hypernasality due to abnormal palatal structures.

Surgical treatment is directed toward advancement of the midface structures and correction of any dental abnormalities. Speech therapy may be best following surgical correction.

Emotional distress

Conversion aphonia: Lack of muscle control of the vocal folds leads to the inability to speak. Persons with this disorder may whisper or produce no sounds at all. After a thorough clinical work up ruling out physical causes, psychotherapy is recommended.

Ventricular dysphonia: The false vocal folds interfere with phonation. The false vocal folds are composed of portions of the arytenoid muscles. There are four known causes of ventricular dysphonia that include obstruction, congenital abnormalities, and overuse syndromes. The fourth cause, the most rare, is due to emotional stress. When the cause is emotional, behavior therapy and psychotherapy are the treatments of choice.

Vocal hyperfunction: Excessive force in the closure of the vocal folds causes hoarseness and vocal fatigue. This disorder is caused by abnormal contraction of the muscles that close the vocal folds and is induced by emotional stress. Yawn-sigh therapy is a technique used to relax the structures of the vocal tract and is used to correct vocal hyperfunction.

Neurogenic Disorders

Apraxia

Apraxia is a disorder in motor planning and voluntary speech movements due to central nervous system injury. There is no motor weakness or muscular disorder present. The congenital form of apraxia found in children is called developmental apraxia of speech. Acquired apraxia can affect a person of any age.

Therapy is essential in recovery, especially in children. One-on-one therapy is important and may include speech movement sequencing, speech imitation, and speed control. The use of pictures to expand vocabulary is helpful. Sign language can be used to enhance oral language and reduce frustration. Therapist often use touch cueing and physical prompting.

Developmental apraxia

Children often make great efforts to speak while having difficulty in placing sounds and syllables in correct order. Consonant, vowel, and word cluster errors are seen.
- Articulation errors are inconsistent.
- There may be incorrect use of speech prosody, whereby the correct use of speech rhythm and infections are improper.
- The ability to understand language is present.
- Spelling and reading difficulties may be present.
- Speech sounds are prolonged and repetitious.
- Children may have problems with phonation and resonance.
- Children may have other problems related to motor coordination, such as feeding, and

may not be able to copy mouth movement or sounds proficiently.

Aphasia

Aphasia is a disorder in language communication due to brain injury. The most common etiologies are stroke, brain tumor, trauma, and infection. Language deficits may be partial or total. Deficits may include a loss of expressive or receptive language; loss of reading skills (alexia), both verbal and comprehensive; or loss writing skills (agraphia). Furthermore, patients may lose the ability to comprehend certain auditory, tactile, or visual stimuli. This deficit is referred to as agnosia. The major categories of aphasia are nonfluent, fluent, and subcortical aphasia. In nonfluent aphasia, speech is agrammatical and choppy and lacks proper flow. In fluent aphasia, speech has normal fluency but lacks appropriate meaning with misuse of words. Subcortical aphasia refers to communication deficits caused by brain injury below the brain cortex, usually in the basal ganglia and thalamus. Those affected by subcortical aphasia will have fluent speech patterns with word-finding deficits and many have associated limb movement disorders.

The treatment of aphasia begins with an adequate assessment. Standardized tests may be used for initial screening to determine the patient's deficits. More specific functional tests are used to further hone in on appropriate therapeutic needs and to address any social or cultural issues that may act as barriers to treatment. Since auditory comprehension is impaired in many patients with aphasia, it is important to recommend vision and hearing tests by qualified health professionals. Treatment is then directed toward improving expressive speech, receptive language, and reading and writing skills when appropriate. Patients may have the ability to name objects or communicate in simple phrases. These individuals may need therapy to improve complex language, narrative discourse, and language prosody. It is important to use tools and language samples that are familiar and personal to the patient.

Apraxia of speech

Apraxia of speech is characterized by the inability to create meaningful language due to lack of voluntary coordination of the oral structures that produce speech. There is a deficit in the synchronization of the muscles rather than of muscle strength. This coordination deficit is inconsistent. This disorder may be acquired or developmental. Acquired apraxia is typically due to damage to the speech areas of the brain (notably the dominant hemisphere), especially those areas that control motor planning. Causes of acquired apraxia include stroke, trauma, and neurological diseases such as Alzheimer's and myasthenia gravis. In developmental apraxia, the cause is unknown. Boys are more often affected than girls are. Patients with this disorder have difficulty placing syllables and words in the correct order; therefore, they produce slow, choppy speech, with poor prosody. Given that patients with apraxia are aware of their disorder, they often appear to be struggling to produce the correct word and phrases.

Dysarthria

Dysarthria is a mechanical speech disorder caused by injury of the central or peripheral nervous system. Persons with dysarthria typically have deficits in the movement of oral structures and the swallowing mechanism. Speech problems associated with dysarthria are:
- Phonation difficulties of voice quality and voice loudness
- Resonance abnormality, namely hypernasality
- Abnormal prosody, namely monotonous pitch and improper speech rate
- Abnormal articulation with slurred speech, voicing errors, and difficulty with fricatives and affricatives

Therapy consists of the strengthening of muscles involved in speech, breath control, and speed control. Clients may improve with speech drills, modeling, and phonetic placement. Prosthetic devices or computer-aided devices may be used in severe cases.

Dysarthria is the inability to produce intelligible speech due to an abnormality in motor function of the speech-producing structures of the mouth or vocal folds. Speech is typically slow and slurred. This articulation defect may be temporary and caused by intoxication, medication side effects, or dental problems. The most common causes of chronic dysarthria are stroke, trauma, tumor, or neurological degenerative diseases, such as myasthenia gravis, ALS, or Parkinson's disease. Unlike apraxia, the speech errors produced in dysarthria are consistent. Determination of specific muscle abnormalities of the mouth or vocal apparatus is important. The patient's ability to perform mouth tasks (e.g., blowing out a candle) or the repetition of syllable and words can help define specific abnormalities and help to direct treatment. The important classifications of dysarthria are ataxic, spastic, flaccid, hyperkinetic, hypokenetic, and unilateral motor neuron dysarthria.

Flaccid dysarthria is caused by injury of the motor neurons of the medulla and posterior pons. This injury causes paralysis of the mouth, palate, and vocal folds and leads to speech that is slurred, has high nasal quality, and is raspy. There may be difficulty with bilabial sounds and sounds that require vibration of the vocal folds.

Ataxic dysarthria is caused by injury to the cerebellum. This injury causes speech with irregular rhythm and that is uncoordinated with breathing. Underarticulated or explosive speech is common.

Spastic dysarthria is caused by damage to upper motor neurons in the pyramidal tract. This damage causes slow, strained, monotonous speech due to impairment of fine motor movements of the mouth and vocal apparatus muscles.
Hypokinetic dysarthria is caused by damage to the basal ganglia, as with patients with Parkinson's disease. Speech is slurred, rapid, and monotonous. The volume of speech decreases progressively at the end of sentences.

Hyperkinetic dysarthria is caused by damage to the frontal lobes and basal ganglia and is typical in patients with Huntington's disease. Speech is characterized by prolonged syllables, and sentences are often interrupted by silence or occasional bursts of speech.

Dementia

Dementia is a slowly progressive decline in cognitive functioning, such that memory, language, and intellectual abilities are impaired. Patients with this syndrome have poor judgment and lose the ability to think abstractly. Later in the condition, patients may suffer hallucinations, delusional thinking, or depression. Language becomes nonfluent, comprehension declines, and patients have difficulty word finding. There is a sharp rise in the prevalence of dementia with advancing age. At ages 65 to 70, 1.4 % of the population has dementia. This

prevalence doubles as age increases. Dementia has dozens of causes but the most common include: Alzheimer's disease, vascular dementia caused by blockages of small arteries in the brain, frontotemporal dementia, tumors, alcohol/substance abuse, injury, infections (HIV, Jakob-Creutzfeldt disease), and neurodegenerative diseases (e. g., Parkinson's disease).

Alzheimer's disease accounts for up to 70% of all causes of dementias. The histological deficit found in these patients is the deposition of protein in the cortical areas of the brain. These patients first present with mild to moderate short-term memory loss with slow progression. Many patients retain their long-term memory. Their ability to perform activities of daily living becomes hampered by loss of intellectual ability, decreased visual spatial perception, and loss of language fluency.

Parkinson's disease results from a disruption in the conduction of the neurotransmitter dopamine within the basal ganglia. Patients with this disease first display movement abnormalities such as poor balance, slow gait, muscle rigidity, slow speech, difficulty swallowing, and tremor. Dementia occurs in the later stages of the disease.

Huntington's is a genetic disease caused by the degeneration of neurons in the frontal lobe and basal ganglia. Huntington's patients display motor deficits typical of uncontrolled, jerky movements (chorea). Speech is slurred and slow. Dementia is an end-stage result.

Frontotemporal dementia (Pick's disease) is caused by the degeneration of cells in the frontal temporal lobes. The deficits are similar to Alzheimer's with the addition of personality changes and often the complete loss of speech.

Assessment and management of dementia

It is important to differentiate reversible causes of dementia from permanent ones. Patients should undergo a full medical screening by a health care professional to rule out treatable causes of dementia. Medical screening includes a thorough medical and social history and pertinent diagnostic tests. It is important to assess the patient's orientation to person, place, and time as well as the ability to recognize familiar people, objects, and place. Also included in the assessment of patients with dementia are their memory, ability to abstract, awareness of spatial relationships, expressive and receptive language, ability to calculate, and ability to perform activities of daily living. Also important is the assessment of mobility and swallowing. A psychological evaluation may also be appropriate. Treatment is based on individual needs and may include speech therapy, physical therapy, safety training, medications, and psychosocial counseling. Family members should play a large part in treatment strategies. Modification of the patient's environment to improve safety and orientation is extremely important.

Dysphagia

Dysphagia is difficulty in swallowing. This difficulty may be associated with pain and caused by any abnormalities along the swallowing pathway, namely, the mouth, tongue, pharynx, or esophagus. Dysfunction of these structures may be caused by intrinsic muscle abnormalities, nerve disruption, infection, or obstruction due to growths. Congenital structural abnormalities, such as cleft palate or jaw malformation, may cause dysphagia as well. These dysfunctions cause loss of mobility or paralysis of swallowing structures or the inability to grind food to a manageable size. Patients with dysphasia may complain of difficulty in swallowing liquids or solid foods freely. They may cough or choke frequently while eating or pool large amounts of foods or liquids in their mouths while eating. They may have similar symptoms while lying down due to the passage of undigested food into the pharynx. Screening for dysphagia should be considered if patients have unexplained weight loss.

Assessment and treatment of dysphagia

- Evaluate the patient's cognitive ability.
- Examine the patient's oral motor function.
- Examine the patient's swallowing mechanics. This evaluation can include the use of an esophagram. In this diagnostic procedure, the patient swallows a substance called barium, and a series of X-rays shows the movement of the fluid from the mouth to the stomach. The esophagram can uncover obstructive, functional, or structural abnormalities.
- Refer patient as appropriate to physician for direct or indirect visualization of the oral, pharyngeal, or esophageal structures.
- Treatment of dysphasia should be directed at optimizing chewing, optimizing head position before and after swallowing, training effective swallowing techniques, modifying the types of food and liquids consumed, and providing therapies to improve oral muscle strength and coordination. Treat any reversible causes of dysphasia, such as infection or

metabolic disturbances. Surgery should be considered when appropriate.

Rancho Scale

The Rancho Scale was developed to rate the level of cognitive functioning in patients suffering from severe brain injury. This scale gives a method of communicating to family members to understand the levels of improvement of cognitive ability as the patient improves. This is helpful for family members with regards to levels of expectations. The family has a better understanding of how to relate to the patient and how best to assist in recovery.

The levels of cognitive functioning on the Rancho Scale are:

- Level I: No response to stimulation: total assistance
- Level II: Generalized response to stimulation: total assistance
- Level III: Localized response to stimulation: total assistance
- Level IV: Confused, agitated behavior: maximal assistance
- Level V: Confused, inappropriate, nonagitated behavior: maximal assistance
- Level VI: Confused, appropriate behavior: moderate assistance
- Level VII: Automatic, appropriate behavior: minimal assistance for daily living skills
- Level VIII: Purposeful, appropriate: stand-by assistance
- Level IX: Purposeful, appropriate: stand-by assistance on request
- Level X: Purposeful, appropriate: modified independent

Melodic intonation therapy (MIT)

Melodic intonation therapy (MIT) is a rehabilitative treatment for individuals with language deficits caused by brain injury, especially in the speech centers in the right brain. This technique uses a type of singing called melodic intonation to improve the neurological connections in the brain involved with speech. Therefore, this would be an appropriate therapy for patients with Broca's aphasia. The treatment begins with the therapist's humming and tapping of intoned phrases and progresses to the patient's joining in. Later, the patient will sing the intoned phrases, repeating the therapist. Finally, the patient will sing the phrases by himself. This type of therapy works best in patients with good attention, auditory comprehension, and emotional stability.

Audiology/Hearing

Hearing loss

Normal hearing occurs within the decibel levels of 20 to 20,000 Hz. Hearing loss occurs when there is a deficit in hearing anywhere along this range. The upper ranges decline with advancing age. The range of normal speech falls between 500 and 4,000 Hz. There are five categories depicting the severity of hearing loss based on the decibel level for which the subject is able to detect sound:

1. Normal hearing: sounds can be detected up to 20 dB
2. Mild hearing loss: 20 to 40 dB
3. Moderate hearing loss: 40 to 60 dB
4. Severe hearing loss: 60 to 80 dB
5. Profound hearing loss: greater than 80 dB

It is important to note if the hearing loss occurs in a single or both ears, whether one ear has greater loss than the other has or whether the loss was sudden or gradual.

Categories of hearing loss

Hearing loss is divided into three categories: conductive, sensorineural, and mixed.

Conductive hearing loss is caused by the disruption of sound waves from the ear canal to the middle ear. This is most commonly caused by impaction of wax in the ear canal. Other causes of conductive hearing loss are middle ear infection (otitis media), eardrum perforation, growths behind the eardrum (cholesteostoma), and middle ear bone abnormalities.

Sensorineural hearing loss is caused by the disruption of sound signals from the cochlear structure of the middle ear to the nerve pathway to the brain. This hearing loss may be acquired or congenital. Causes of acquired sensorineural hearing loss include infection, tumor, stroke, medications, presbyacusis (age-related hearing loss), and trauma.

Mixed hearing loss is a combination of the two.

Auditory processing disorder

Auditory processing disorder is impairment in the management of auditory signals transmitted to the brain. Individuals with this disorder have deficits in understanding spoken words. This is most profound when the environment is noisy and unstructured. Other features include difficulty distinguishing like-sounding words, lack of focus for the details of spoken language, poor memory for auditory details, and difficulty comprehending oral abstract language. Children may have difficulty with writing and reading information presented to them verbally. Auditory processing disorder may result from congenital or acquired causes. Acquired causes are typically due to infections or trauma. This disorder is commonly diagnosed at age 7 or 8 because the younger brain is still developing in its ability to process auditory information. Treatment is aimed at improving the learning environment, such as using visual prompts and therapy to target specific auditory processing deficits.

Retrocochlear disorders

Retrocochlear disorders refer to abnormalities that disrupt the connection between the cochlear area of the hearing apparatus and the brain stem. Tumors, blood vessel abnormalities, and infections are among the most common causes of retrocochlear hearing loss. Acoustic neuromas and neurofibromatosis are the types of tumors typically seen. Acoustic neuromas, the most common type of retrocochlear tumor, are benign tumors that develop from the Schwann cells of cranial nerve 8. These tumors may grow to sizes significant enough to compress surrounding structures, such as the cerebellum, blood vessels, and other cranial nerves. Persons with these tumors will complain of unilateral hearing loss, ear ringing, headache, and vertigo. Neurofibromatosis, another cause of retrocochlear tumors is a genetic growth of benign tumors on nerves. When the cranial nerve 8 is involved, hearing deficits occur. The signs and symptoms are similar to those found in acoustic neuromas.

Hearing assessment in infants and young children

The detection of hearing loss in infancy is important in that hearing impairments negatively affect language and speech acquisition. Testing in the first 3 months of life is recommended to prevent speech development delays. Children who have experienced intrauterine complications, birth trauma, or low birth weight or who have genetic predispositions or autism are at greatest risk of hearing impairments. Given the obvious difficulty in assessing infants and young children for hearing deficits, modalities other than standard audiometry are used. The use of localization techniques is most common. A sound-producing object, such as a rattle or bell, is placed near the child. A normal response is the turning of the head toward the sound. Most recently, clinicians have exploited the presence of auditory brain stem response in hearing. Electrodes placed on the scalp of infants can show brainwave responses to sounds.

Tuning fork

A tuning fork is a 2-pronged fork made of metal. Formerly used by musicians to tune instruments, the tuning fork is used by clinicians to assess hearing. In the Weber test, a tuning fork (usually tuned to 512 hz) is struck and placed on the mastoid bone behind the ear. When the sound is no longer audible, it is placed near the ear. The sound of the tuning fork at the ear should last twice that of bone. In persons with conductive hearing loss, bone conduction is better than air conduction. In the Rinne test, the tuning fork is placed on the forehead or teeth and the sound is transmitted in the center of the head normally. In conductive hearing loss, sound is transmitted to the effected ear. In sensorineural hearing loss, sound is referred away from the effected ear.

Devices used in hearing evaluations

A clinician's physical examination of the head structures is the first step in the evaluation of hearing deficits. Audiometry is the standard device used to identify hearing deficits. An examiner uses a machine (audiometer) that produces sounds within specified spectrums. Earphones are place on the subject who is in a soundproof environment. The subject is asked if each sound is detected. Pure tone air audiometry testing measures hearing ability to different pitches and volumes. Speech audiometry measures hearing ability to spoken words. This involves volume and discrimination of words and sounds. Tympanometry is used to measure movement of the eardrum in response to auditory stimuli at various frequencies. This method is used to detect abnormalities of the middle ear, such as infection or middle ear obstruction. Clinicians may also use brain-imaging technologies, such as MRI and CT scans, to detect structural abnormalities.

Speech disorders

Lack of adequate modeling can cause profound problems in the production of speech. The severity of the speech disorder is highly dependent on the extent of hearing loss. Children with congenital hearing impairment experience speech disorders more profoundly than those with postlingual hearing impairment do. The phonological errors that are typical in the hearing impaired include omissions of initial and final consonants, especially the /s/ sounds; the nasalization of consonants; vowel prolongation and mispronunciations; and alteration of all sounds, with fricatives and stops being most often altered. The hearing impaired may exhibit speech that is less complex and less abstract than the speech of those with normal hearing. Abnormalities may exist in the rhythm, rate, and loudness of speech. There are typically resonance problems, with an inappropriate amount of nasal resonance found in particular sounds.

Aural rehabilitation

Aural rehabilitation is a program to assist hearing-impaired persons to function in their environment. This program involves participation among family, audiologists, and clinicians. After the assessment of the client's needs, interventions are directed at improving home, work, school, or recreational activities. Aural rehabilitation typically includes a determination of appropriate amplification devices, such as hearing aids, cochlear implants, and telecommunication equipment. Communication training is a large part of aural rehabilitation. This may involve both verbal and nonverbal methods of communication, such as sign language. Financial considerations must be taken into account. A review of the patient's financial resources and access to clinical care must be considered when advising a plan. Be aware of the client's motivation to rehabilitation and ability to carry out planned services. Identify any emotional issues that may require therapy.

Hearing aids

Hearing aids are electronic devices that amplify sounds and are used to improve hearing and language. There are three main categories of hearing aids.

In behind-the-ear models, the electronics are in a plastic case that is located behind the ear while the conductive piece fits at the opening of the ear canal.

The in-the-ear models fit inside the ear. These devices are not recommended for younger clients, given that children's ears grow continuously.

The in-the-canal and completely-in-the-canal devices are very small and are placed within the ear canal. Given that these canal devices are very small, they may not be appropriate for those who have difficulty with finger manipulation, as they may be difficult to insert, remove, and adjust. Also, their small size limits their power, and they may not be adequate for severe hearing impairment. Furthermore, these canal devices are inappropriate for growing children.

Following the correct fitting of the hearing aid, clients are then properly trained to recognize amplified sounds.

Communication training

Auditory training is used to recognize amplified sounds emitted via hearing aids. There are many situations, such as a classroom or lecture hall, when hearing aids may not be optimal. To decrease background noise, an auditory trainer can be used. This is a portable device in which the client uses headphones while the speaker's voice is transmitted via a microphone. There are wireless auditory trainers available.

Speech reading or lip reading is a viable part of communication training but best when coupled with other forms of communication.

Cued speech is a system communication that uses a small set of hand signals to represent letters. This is used as a supplement to lip reading and was developed to improve the recognition of different phonemes.

Oral language training and voice training is used to improve articulation, volume, speech rate, and intonation.

Language training in young clients should include grammar, pragmatics, definitions, and abstracts of language.

Clinical Management

Assessment of persons with suspected language disorders

- Screen subjects using a formal and/or informal testing procedure to determine if a more detailed assessment is warranted.
- Obtain a description of the problem from the subject (if appropriate), caregivers, teachers, and health professionals. Determine if there have been any prior treatments.
- Interview caregivers, family members, and peers to obtain information about the nature of the speech and language ability of the subject.
- Observe the family communication style. Make note of social interactions and languages spoken.
- Obtain a health history of the mother and subject, including the prenatal and postnatal periods and childhood developmental history.
- Obtain educational history and occupational history of adults.
- Examine hearing and screen for any oral-facial defects.
- Obtain speech and language samples from the subject.

Standardized (formal) tests used for language assessment

Advantages of standardized tests
- They provide comparison data with age-matched peers.
- They provide a measurement that will be consistent across all examiners.

Disadvantages of standardized tests
- Data obtained may not be applicable to some segments of the population that are linguistically and culturally diverse.
- Certain characteristics of language may not be tested in all contexts or situations.
- They cannot be used as a single source of assessing children's language skills or assigning treatment strategies.

Nonstandardized (informal) tests for language assessment

Criterion-referenced testing: This method of assessment takes into account individual-specific context of language, such as culture. Instead of standard target goals, baseline behaviors are established for the subject, and individualized goals are established.

Authentic assessment subjects are evaluated via their performance of a given task.

Dynamic assessment is a type of authentic assessment whereby the individual is provided with directions on how to perform a task, and the ability to perform the task is assessed.

Portfolio assessment is a type of authentic assessment whereby a body of the individual's performance ability is collected over time. The subject is given directions on how to perform a task, and the development of the performance is observed over time.

Functional or social assessment: Information on speech and language is obtained from peers, teachers, caregivers, and health professionals. The subject is examined in various social settings, and this information is used in treatment.

Type-token ratio

The type-token ratio (TTR) measures children's lexical diversity or their variety of expressive words used in conversation. Measuring TTR:

- TTR = <u>Number of different words in a sample</u> (a word counts only once if repeated)
- Number of words in a sample (count even if word is repeated)

The typical value of TTR for children ages 3 to 8 is 0.5, or 1:2 ratio. TTR can be applied only to children ages 3 to 8. This is in contrast to the mean length utterance (MLU) analysis of children's language, which can be applied to children of any age.

Assessment of speech and language for infants and toddlers (<3 years)

- Assess the child's readiness for speech.
- Identify any medical problems that would affect the child's attention status.
- Identify any hearing deficits.
- Assess the child's developmental milestones: cognitive, motor, social, and speech.
- Collect relevant information about the child's language from caregivers and teachers.
- Observe caregiver-child interactions. The Mother-Infant Play Interaction Scale is a standardized test that is used to assess the caregiver's interaction style and the child's response to the interaction stimulus.
- Observe the child's play interactions with other children.

Assessing cognitive, social, and motor development of infants and toddlers

Denver Developmental Screening Test is used to assess the developmental progress of children. It encompasses many areas of development, including cognitive, motor, emotional, behavioral, and language. This test can be used to identify many learning disabilities. It is used to screen children from birth to 6 years.

The Communication Screen is used to assess auditory and verbal comprehension in children ages 2 to 5 years.

Bayley Scale of Infant Mental Development is a psychological test used to assess the mental, behavioral, and motor development of children from birth to 2.5 years.

Battelle Developmental Inventory is used to assess five areas of developmental achievements in children 6 months to 8 years. These areas are social, adaptive behavior, psychomotor, cognitive, and communication.

Vineland Adaptive Behavior Scale is used to assess the socialization skills in children from birth through 18 months. Included in this test are measures of receptive/expressive language and gross/fine motor skills.

Assessing speech and language in infants and toddlers

Preschool Language Scale is used to assess receptive and expressive language skills in children ages 2 weeks to 6 years. Both caregivers and children are interviewed to obtain appropriate data for assessment.

Early Language Milestone Scale-2 is used to determine speech and language skills in children from birth through 3 years. It can assess expressive, auditory, visual, and receptive language.

Receptive-Expressive Emergent Language Test-3 (REEL-2) is a 132-item checklist of language milestones that is provided by the child's caregiver. This test is used to assess children from birth through 3 years.

Assessing speech and language for preschool and elementary-age children

- Assess children for language disorders using nonstandardized methods or standardized screening tests.
- Determine problems with comprehension of complex language.
- Determine the presence of delay of expressive speech or poor vocabulary.
- Observe problems with word meaning, vocabulary, word structure, syntactic development, pragmatic skills, and comprehension.
- Use pictures and narratives to evoke language responses for assessment.
- Obtain information from caregivers and teachers.
- Observe family interactions and communication methods.

Denver Developmental Screening Test is used to assess the developmental progress of children. It encompasses many areas of development, including cognitive, motor, emotional, behavioral, and language. This test can be used to identify many learning disabilities. It is used to screen children from birth to 6 years.

The Communication Screen is used to assess auditory and verbal

comprehension in children ages 2 to 5 years.

Preschool Language and Screening Test-4 is used to assess receptive and expressive language, social communication, and voice disorders in children ages 3 to 5.5 years.

Bankson Language Screening Test is used to assess speech morphology, syntax, and pragmatics in children ages 3 to 7.

Fluharty Preschool Speech and Language Screening Test-3 is used to identify communication problems in children ages 2 to 6. Children's ability to articulate, repeat sentences, follow directions, answer questions, describe actions, and sequence events is assessed.

Assessing expressive and receptive language in preschool and elementary-age children

The Peabody Picture Vocabulary Test assesses the receptive vocabulary in children 2.5 years through adult through the ability to identify pictures and illustrations following a verbal stimulus.

The Receptive One-Word Picture Vocabulary Test provides an evaluation of children's (ages 35 months through 12 years old) receptive single-word vocabulary. The child is given a one-word stimulus and he must identify the picture accordingly.

The Expressive One-Word Picture Vocabulary Test provides an evaluation of children's (ages 35 months through 12 years old) expressive single-word vocabulary. Children demonstrate their ability to name objects and concepts in illustrated pictures.

The Test of Word Finding-2 is used to assess children's ability to name pictures depicting objects or actions.

The Test of Auditory Comprehension of Language-3 tests children's receptive language in the categories of vocabulary, grammar, and sentence structure. This test is used for children ages 3 to 9.

The Test of Early Language Development-3 assesses the receptive and expressive language in children ages 2-7. This version of the test is reported to be applicable to all races, genders, and socioeconomic status.

The Token Test for Children is to assess the development in children aged 3 to 12.5 of receptive language. In this test, auditory reception and processing and discrimination of speech sounds are evaluated.

Assessing syntax, morphology, and semantics of language in preschool and elementary-age children

Assessment of Children's Language Comprehension tests children's comprehension of word classes in various combinations of length and complexity. This test, used for children 3 to 7 years old, measures receptive vocabulary and syntax.

Clinical Evaluation of Language Fundamentals-4 is used to assess receptive and expressive language, language structure and memory, morphology, and syntax. This test is useful for subjects from ages 5 through adult.

Multilevel Informal Language Inventory measures children's expressive ability to produce semantic relations, syntactical structures, and language morphology. It is used in children ages 4 through 12.

Test of Language Development Primary-3 is used in the assessment of multiple aspects of spoken language, including vocabulary, comprehension, grammar, and sentence structure. Both receptive and expressive forms of language are assessed. This test is used in children ages 4 to 9.

Assessing preschool and elementary-age children

Boehm Test of Basic Concepts-3 is used to assess language skills of children from kindergarten through 3rd grade. Children are asked to identify pictures of relational concepts, such as size and position.

Detroit Test of Learning and Aptitude: Primary-3 is used to assess the verbal, attention, and visual motor aspects of cognition in children ages 3 to 10.

Test for Examining Expressive Morphology is a brief test used to assess the development of expressive morphemes in children ages 3 to 7.

Test for Pragmatic Skills is used for children ages 3 to 9 who are suspected of having an impaired or absence of conversational language. In this test, illustrations of situations are presented, and children are asked to respond. This may give the examiner insight into the child's social knowledge and pragmatic language development.

Token Test for Children is a specialized test used to assess the development of receptive language in children ages 3 to 12.5. In this test, children's auditory reception, auditory processing, and discrimination of speech sounds are evaluated.

Assessing speech and language in adolescents

- Screen for any language problems with use of standardized and nonstandardized methods.
- Observe for syntactical errors or lack of speech fluency.
- Observe the child's range of vocabulary and ability to maintain conversational discourse.
- Evaluate the child's comprehension of words, figurative language, and abstract concepts.
- Determine if any reading and writing abnormalities exist. Specifically, observe letter formation, sentence structure, organization, and grammatical content.
- Interview caregivers, teachers, and peers about the child's language.
- Observe children in the classroom to identify any specific behaviors that may disrupt learning.
- Determine whether one-on-one, small group, classroom intervention, or a combination may be suitable for the child.

Screening for Adolescent Language is a rapid screening test for children ages 11 to 18 to identify abnormalities in vocabulary, auditory memory, language processing, and comprehension of figurative language.

Clinical Evaluation of Language Fundamentals is a comprehensive screening test for children ages 5 to 16. It analyzes children's receptive and expressive speech, language morphology, semantic knowledge, syntax, pragmatics, memory, logic, and attention.

Classroom Communication Screening Procedure for Early Adolescents was developed to determine the cognitive and communication skills required for secondary education. It is used to screen children ages 9 to 14 in their development of verbal expression and their ability to follow directions.

Adolescent Language Screening is used to screen children ages 11 to 17 in their development of expressive/receptive language, pragmatics, morphology, and syntactic and semantic language skills.

Assessing syntax, morphology, and semantics of language in adolescents

Clinical Evaluation of Language Fundamentals-4 is used to assess receptive/expressive language, language structure and memory, morphology, and syntax. This test is useful for subjects from age 5 through adult.

Bilingual Syntax Measure is used to measure linguistic proficiency in children at the 3rd through 12th grade level in both English and Spanish.

The Word Test: Adolescent is used to assess expressive vocabulary and semantics in children ages 12 to 18. Children are asked to demonstrate their knowledge of language and word meanings in ordinary and exceptional situations.

Test of Problem Solving: Adolescent is used to assess expressive language, cognition, and problem-solving skills in children ages 12 to 18. In this test, a series of open-ended questions is used to elicit responses.

Fullerton Language Test for Adolescents measures the receptive and expressive language skills in subjects ages 11 to adult. In this test, language morphology, syntax, and semantics are assessed.

Assessing written language in adolescents

Woodcock Language Proficiency Battery is used to assess oral vocabulary, reading, and writing proficiency in subjects ages 11 to adult.

Test of Adolescent and Adult Language-4 is used to assess expressive and written language abilities in subjects of ages 12 to 25. Specific concepts covered in this test are analogies, opposites, similarities, word meanings, sentence structure, and punctuation.

Assessimg naming and vocabulary skills in adolescents

Expressive One-Word Picture Vocabulary Test: Upper Extension provides an evaluation of receptive single-word vocabulary in children ages 12 to 16. The child is given a one-word stimulus and must identify the picture accordingly.

Receptive One-Word Picture Vocabulary Test: Upper Extension provides an evaluation of expressive single-word vocabulary in children ages 12 to 16. Children demonstrate their ability to name objects and concepts through illustrations.

Test of Adolescent/Adult Word Finding assesses the subject's ability in word finding with regard to speed and accuracy. Examinees are tested on nouns, verbs, sentence completion, descriptions, and concept categories. This test can be used to assess subjects from age 12 to adult.

Treatment of articulation-phonation disorders

The motor-based approaches to the treatment of articulation and phonation disorders presume that children have motor and perceptual defects with regard to speech sound production. These approaches are best used with children who have only several errors in phoneme production; do not have severe articulation deficits; and whose articulation disorder is based on physical insufficiencies.

The most frequently used motor-based approaches are:
- Van Riper's traditional approach
- McCabe and Bradley's multiple-phoneme approach
- Baker and Ryan's Monterey Articulation Program
- McDonald's sensory approach
- Irwin and Weston's paired-stimuli approach

Traditional approaches to articulation-phonation therapy

Van Riper's traditional approach emphasizes phonetic placement (teaching sounds of phonemes by instruction, modeling, and physical guidance); auditory discrimination/perceptual training (teaching the distinction between correct and incorrect speech sounds); and repetition of isolated speech sounds.

McCabe and Bradley's multiple-phoneme approach is based on Van Riper's traditional approach except that more than one speech sound is addressed and all problematic speech sounds are addressed in each session. Three phases are employed:
1. Establishment of the correct sound in response to a symbol for that sound
2. Transfer of target sounds to different situations
3. Maintenance of accuracy of sound production in various situations and conversation

Baker and Ryan's Monterey Articulation Program

Baker and Ryan's Monterey Articulation Program involves programmed conditioning to treat articulation disorders. This approach is based on behavioral therapy principles that speech sounds are learned motor behaviors. Sounds are targeted via a program of steps. These targeted sounds are then generalized to home and classroom, and finally maintenance therapy is employed. Since repetition of motor skills is emphasized, the approach is best for children requiring a structured motor-articulation program.

McDonald's sensory approach to articulation-phonological therapy

McDonald's sensory approach involves speech training at the level of the syllable, and not the phoneme. Perceptual training is not emphasized, but the phonetic environment is important. Practice begins with bisyllabic and trisyllabic sounds that are not in error. Correct pronunciation of sounds that are in error are trained and then moved to more varied contexts and then to natural communication.

Instrumental methods used in the visualization of the vocal folds

Indirect laryngoscopy: the use of a specialized mirror by a medical specialist to examine the larynx. Vocal cord movement can be assessed during speech.

Direct laryngoscopy: the examination of the larynx with a laryngoscope by a medical specialist. This procedure is done under anesthesia. Given that the patient cannot speak, this procedure is best when a biopsy is needed rather than for assessment of vocal cord movement.

Flexible fiberoptic laryngoscopy: the introduction of a flexible laryngoscope by a specialist through the nose to examine the laryngeal structures. Vocal movements can be viewed via a fiberoptic light system.

Rigid and flexible endoscopy: Also performed by a specialist, rigid endoscopy employs the use of a nonflexible camera that is introduced via the mouth. Unlike the flexible scope, the rigid endoscope may be passed further to the level of the laryngeal mechanism. The flexible endoscope (nasopharyngeoscope) is introduced via the nose to the velopharyngeal area. With endoscopy, fine vocal structures as well as vocal movement can be visualized.

Assessing the quality of movement of the vocal folds

Spectrography analyzes speech through measurements of amplitude and frequencies. This is most frequently used to determine the effectiveness of treatment of a voice disorder.

The videostroboscopic method uses an instrument called a videostroboscope that emits a pulsating light that creates slow-motion viewing of the vocal folds. This device can be attached to a rigid endoscope or flexible fiber-optic endoscopy. The images detail the movement of the vocal structures and can determine the presence of tumors.

Electroglottography (EGG) is used to monitor vocal vibration and closure patterns. This study is noninvasive and uses electrodes that attach to the neck.

Electromyography (EMG) assesses the activity of the muscles of the vocal folds. This is useful in diagnosing vocal cord neuromuscular disorders.

Spirometry or plethysmography is used to measure lung and breath volumes.

Hypernasality and hyponasality

Hypernasality treatment: Biofeedback is used to raise the subject's awareness of nasal resonance. A nasometer is a device that gives subjects feedback on the presence of nasality in speech production. Visual and auditory cues can be used to monitor production of nasal sounds. Therapy is directed at improving mouth opening, articulation, pitch, rate, and loudness to appropriate levels.

Hyponasality treatment: Nasometer feedback and visual and auditory cues are used to monitor correct sound production. Therapy is directed at training the subject to focus the pronunciation of appropriate words toward the nasal in an exaggerated way. Therapy also includes practicing the production of nasal and glide phonemes in combination. Feedback is then used so that the subject can determine proper nasalization.

Admission and discharge of clients within a speech pathology practice

Referrals for services may come from clinicians, educators, caregivers, family members, clients, or county agencies. Criteria for admission to services include:

- Presence of a communication deficit where there is a clear difference in communication among peers, a disruption of education, socialization, or employment, or the presence of a health and safety hazard
- Presence of a swallowing deficit in which there is a negative effect on nutrition, health, and safety
- It is appropriate to discharge clients from services under the following conditions:
- All language and communication or swallowing goals are met or the client's skills meet standards that

are comparable to his or her peers.
- The client has reached the maximum benefits of therapy or is unable to progress due to clinical or emotional reasons.
- A Request for discharge by caregivers or legal guardians or a change of provider or location has been made.
- The client is unwilling to participate or has aberrant behavior hampering continued services.

Record keeping

The speech-language pathologist has the responsibility to keep accurate records of all clients. The records should contain identifying information about the client (e.g., name, address, referring agency). Contact and pertinent information about family, clinical providers, and educators should be found in the records. The speech-language pathologist should document all issues of the screening examination, communication, speech, language and swallowing deficits. Details of all training sessions should include the date and times of sessions. Treatment plans should be included and detail all goals. Client's responses to treatment should be recorded. Records are typically the property of hospitals, clinics, referring agencies, and schools when appropriate. Records should be kept in a safe place so that confidentiality is maintained. A written consent by the client or guardian is required for outside agencies or persons to obtain the contents of these records.

Diadochokinetic rate

The diadochokinetic rate is used to assess children's oral motor skills. The ability to produce rapid speech movements using various parts of the oral structures is determined. Children who are unable to make these rapid speech movements typically have a difficult time sequencing speech sounds. A group of syllables or words is given to the child to pronounce and repeat rapidly. These syllables or words are important in that they use a combination of mouth structures (e.g., lips, tongue, palate) to pronounce. Two common groups of sounds used are *puh-tuh-kuh* and *patty cake*. These two words use syllables that require the lips, tongue, and palate to pronounce in sequence. Children are asked to repeat these words as many times as they can in a set amount of time, usually 5 seconds. A score is given based on age-appropriate standards. One of the most common tests that uses diadochokinesis is the Fletcher Time-by-Count Test of Diadochokinetic Syllable Rate.

Assessing articulation

Goldman-Fristoe Test of Articulation is used to assess the articulation of consonant sounds in children and young adults. This test is best for subjects of ages 2 to 21.

Fischer-Logemann Test of Articulation Competence is used to assess the ability to articulate all phonemes. It is used for subjects from preschool through adulthood and is practical for regional and ethnic dialects.

McDonald Deep Test is used to determine the various contexts in which sounds are misarticulated. It uses a series of pictures, which makes it suitable for children.

The Arizona Articulation Proficiency Scale is a contextual, picture-driven articulation test for children. It is like the McDonald Deep but more contemporary.

Templin-Darley Test is used to assess the articulation skills of subjects ages 3 to adult.

Assessing individuals with neurological speech disorders

Scales of Cognitive Ability for Traumatic Brain Injury (SCATBI) is used to assess the cognitive ability of individuals from adolescence to adulthood.

The Western Aphasia Battery (WAB) is used to assess the language skills of adults with aphasia due to acquired brain injury. This test is so comprehensive that it is often used to assist in the diagnosis of the type of neurological brain injury present. It contains a nonverbal component for testing as well.

Mini-inventory of Right Brain Injury (MIRBI) is used to determine the types of language deficits present in individuals with right brain injuries and can be used in individuals ages 20 to 80.

Ross Information Processing Assessment (RIPA)is used to determine the level of cognitive and language deficits present in adults with neurological brain disorders. Communication Activities of Daily Living (CADL) is used to assess functional language ability in adults with neurological-based language abnormalities.

Bedside Evaluation & Screening Test (BEST) is used to assess the language abilities in adults with aphasia.

Apraxia Battery For Adults (ABA) measures the presence and severity of apraxia in adults by way of performance assessment of a series of tasks.

Frenchay Dysarthria Assessment is used to measure the presence and severity of dysarthria in adults.

Individualized education program (IEP) for children with disabilities

The individualized education program (IEP) was developed as part of the Individuals with Disabilities Education Act (IDEA). It mandates school districts and local educational agencies to develop periodic sets of goals for the treatment of children from ages 3 to 18 and to follow the implementing of those goals. This program is usually instituted by the individual school districts of each state. It begins with the identification of any child with special needs, following a thorough evaluation. The child must meet eligibility requirements authorized by the county or state to receive services. All parties responsible for the child's care meet to plan special needs services and goals for the following months. Individuals at the meeting include school district officials, therapists, social service workers, teachers, and caregivers. The progress of the child is reassessed, and another meeting takes place in 1 year or less to adjust goals and treatment.

Reinforcers

A positive reinforcer is a reward that the child enjoys. She receives the reinforcer when she performs a desired behavior. A primary positive reinforcer is something that the child already enjoys. For a secondary positive reinforcer, the child has to learn to derive some benefit from it. The reinforcer can be provided at a fixed rate (e.g., every 10 minutes) or at a variable rate. It can also be provided via a ratio formula or a variable ratio formula whereby the child receives the reinforcer if she performs the behavior a particular number of times. The reinforcer can also be administered at random. When a reinforcer fails to stimulate the desired behavior, it is called extension. A variable schedule of reinforcement should prevent this. Negative reinforcers enhance a behavior by taking away something that is unpleasant for the child in response to the desired behavior.

Professional Issues, Psychometrics, and Research

Certification

The current requirements for certification for speech-language pathology were implemented in 2005. All applicants applying after January 1, 2006, must adhere to these requirements regardless of when the coursework for certification was completed. Applicants must possess a master's, doctoral, or appropriate postbaccalaureate degree to apply for certification. Graduate course work and clinical participation must be attended at a program that is approved by the Council on Academic Accreditation in Audiology and Speech-Language Pathology. The graduate degree may be in any area of study, but the applicant must complete a minimum of 75 semester credits in areas pertinent to speech and language pathology. The graduate program will determine which courses are appropriate for study. A transcript will be required from the academic facility to demonstrate that these requirements have been met.

Postgraduate certification

The candidate for certification for speech-language pathology must pass the PRAXIS speech-language certification examination with a passing grade of at least 600. For scores to be considered for certification, the examination must have been taken within 5 years of applying for certification. Candidates must also complete a speech-language pathology clinical fellowship following the completion of all course work and practical supervised hours. There must be 36 weeks of completed full-time clinical practice that includes direct patient contact and all administrative duties. There should be 35 hours per week of clinical work under the auspices of a certified speech-language pathologist. A mentor must directly observe 18 hours of the clinical fellowship. The mentor then uses this observation to submit the candidate's assessment. The candidate should be prepared to verify the clinical hours submitted.

Course work and practical requirements

All applicants are required to complete a minimum of 75 semester or 115 quarter hours of appropriate course work. These hours must include at least 36 semester or 47 quarter hours of graduate level course work. There are four areas of course work required: behavioral science, mathematics, biology, and physiology. The academic program will determine the specific subjects that are required in each area. Candidates for certification must also complete 400 hours of supervised clinical experience in speech-language pathology. The requirement is that 25 hours be observation and 375 hours direct client contact. At least 325 of the required 400 hours must have been completed at the graduate level. The applicant may use 75 hours obtained as an undergraduate to complete the requirements. Supervision of clinical experience must be with a certified speech-language pathologist.

Scope of practice

The practice of speech-language pathology involves:
- Screening, assessment, diagnosis, treatment, and prevention of the following disorders: speech (articulation, fluency, resonance, and voice disorders), language (morphology, phonology, syntax, semantics, and pragmatics) both

- oral and written, swallowing, and the cognitive aspects of communication
- Screening for hearing loss and providing services to individuals with hearing loss
- Establishing needs for communication and swallowing devices and assisting in the use of those devices
- Client advocating in community and educational programs to promote improvement in speech, language, or swallowing deficits
- Cooperating with families, educators, and other health professionals to provide consultative services on behalf of the client
- Providing specialized services, such as accent training, voice training to transgender clients, and voice training to improve professional standards
- Using instruments to visualize the oral and vocal structures

American Speech-Language-Hearing Association (ASHA)

The American Speech-Hearing-Language Association (ASHA) was formed to adopt and maintain standards of excellence in the practice of speech-language pathology and audiology. Its organization provides credentialing in these two areas of practice. The Certificate of Clinical Competence is required to practice speech-language pathology and audiology in most states. The intention of ASHA is to prepare competent candidates to provide services to speech- and hearing–impaired individuals. It seeks to encourage scientific study to assist in the diagnosis, treatment, and prevention of communication disorders. Practicing speech pathologists rely on ASHA for updated practice standards. The organization advocates for the speech and hearing impaired and works with those organizations that have similar goals. ASHA acts as a legal and administrative supportive body for those within the profession.

The American Speech-Language-Hearing Association (ASHA) has a strict code of behaviors with regard to providing services in speech, language, and hearing. This standard is expected of all certified and noncertified members of ASHA as well as all applicants and candidates for certification.

The four principles of ethics are as followed:

1. Speech pathologists shall maintain the highest regard for the welfare of their clients. They shall not discriminate on any basis, including race, sexual orientation, or gender. Research shall be conducted in a humane and ethical manner.
2. Pathologists should maintain the highest level of clinical competence.
3. Pathologists should not misrepresent the profession to the public by making inaccurate representations about credentials or making false statements in assessment of clients.
4. Pathologists should maintain truthful and honorable relationships with colleagues and clients.

Health Insurance Portability and Accountability Act of 1996 (HIPAA)

The federal government adopted a set of rules protecting the privacy of patients' medical information while allowing the necessary flow of medical information needed to provide adequate care. Although the statue was written in 1996, the final modifications took effect in April

2003. The law sets standards for health plans and health care providers to provide privacy of patient records that are oral, electronic, or paper. Patients may have access to copies of their medical records upon request and be allowed to add corrections when appropriate. Access must be granted within 30 days. Providers must give patients written notification of how their records will be used. Health practitioners are allowed to share medical information among themselves in the treatment of patients. Signed consent must be obtained to share information with third parties. Medical information may not be shared for marketing purposes. All communication with the patients must be private.

Evidence-based practice in treating communication disorders

There is a continuous amount of clinical research in the area of communication disorders. Institutions use research to provide the best methods of practice in speech pathology. It is important to be able to adequately interpret the large amount of research available and to determine which body of evidence is best applied to clinical practice. There are several important factors important in reviewing the validity of a study. The results of the study should be able to stand up to independent confirmation based on the evidence provided. The study should contain experimental controls and should be unbiased. The size of the samples in the study should be large enough that the results did not occur just by chance. The study should provide information that is relevant and practical to the targeted population.

Experimental design

Experiments in medicine and speech pathology are designed to determine the effect of some treatment or procedure.

The dependent variable of a design is that effect that has been altered by some factor, namely the independent variable. The experimenter must test the treatment or independent variable in an environment free of outside biases. These biases are called confounders. For example, when determining the effect of a speech therapy, a subject's lack of ability to understand English may bias the study. The two main categories of experimental designs are group and single-subject designs. Group designs involve randomizing a group to receive the treatment and one that does not. The two groups are then compared for cause and effects. If used properly, group designs are very accurate. However, it can be very difficult to randomize the two groups accurately. Single-subject designs do not use controls. Instead, they follow the extensive effects of treatment on individuals. It is easier to integrate this design into clinical practice; however, it may be difficult to generalize the results to the general population.

Assessing data from a clinical study

A clinical trial or clinical experiment should be assessed for internal and external validity. Internal validity is present if a causal relationship is established between a treatment and an effect. External validity is present if the causal relationship established can hold up among different settings and groups. Evidence-based practice relies on establishing levels of evidence to interpret clinical studies. There are three general categories of clinical evidence.

Class I evidence refers to data obtained from a randomized controlled experiment. This is considered the best category of evidence.

Class II evidence refers to data obtained from nonrandomized trials or case

- 53 -

studies. The lack of randomization limits reliability of the data from this class.

Class III evidence refers to data obtained from expert opinions or committees. Data from this class is the weakest because of the lack of control group comparisons.

Scales of measurement used to characterize data in a clinical study

Ordinal scale rates a variable of study based on its classification into ordered qualitative categories. Examples of variables on an ordinal scale are restaurant star rankings and numeric perceptions of pain.

Nominal scale contains categories of variables that have no rankings. Examples of nominal variables are political affiliation and country of origin.

Interval scale classifies variables into quantitative categories; however, the variables are compared on a finite interval scale of measurement. Since there is no true zero point, one cannot make a conclusion of how many times higher a variable is compared to another. An example of an interval measurement is temperature on the Fahrenheit scale.

Ratio scale is similar to an interval scale except that it has true zero points, and with it is possible to make mathematic comparisons of the data. An example of a ratio measurement is the Kelvin scale of temperature.

Descriptive (observational) studies

In quantitative research, the goal is to assess the relationship between a set of variables. In descriptive or observational studies, the variables are not changed or manipulated. The measurement of an outcome is made on an observational basis. Types of descriptive studies are:

- Case study: a collection of data on single subjects
- Prospective/cohort study: a measurement of data at the start of a study and after its conclusion; for example, studying the effects of cholesterol in a high-fat diet
- Case control/retrospective study: study of a particular attribute in a group and then comparing variables with a group without the attribute (control group)

Experimental or longitudinal studies.

In experimental or longitudinal studies, data are quantified following some intervention. Types of longitudinal studies are:

- Time series: A variable is measured before and after an intervention.
- Crossover design: This is similar to time series except there are two groups compared for the study. One group receives the treatment while the other receives a reference or placebo treatment. This design is to minimize the effect of other variables that may change the outcome of treatment as is often seen with the time series studies.
- Randomized control design: This is like the crossover design. Two groups are used, but the participants of the two groups are randomized.
- Single-blind study In this study, the subjects do not know the group to which they have been randomized.
- Double-blind study: Here, neither the subjects nor the experimenters know which groups are receiving the real treatment and which are receiving placebo.

Validity and reliability that standardized tests should meet to ensure the absence of test bias

Construct validity is the ability of a test to accurately measure an observable trait. Concurrent validity is the ability of a test to obtain the same measure of results compared to other tests that are already deemed valid.

Content validity is the ability of a test to measure all aspects of an observable trait.

Predictive validity is the ability to predict behavior based on the results of the test.

Test-retest reliability is the consistency of the test to perform the same when given multiple times.

Parallel forms reliability refers to the presence of pretest and posttest forms so that measures of successfulness of a treatment are not biased by memory of test material.

Inter-rater reliability refers to the use of multiple observers to rate the data obtained on a test. This affords more reliability of the data obtained.

Using standardized tests in order to minimize their inherent disadvantages

Attempt to use standardized tests that are norm-referenced. Norm-referenced tests are those in which scores from a sample group of subjects is analyzed such that the individual being tested is compared to a sample of his peers.
- Evaluate the standardized test for validity and reliability.
- Give details for all incorrect responses on the test.
- Use nonstandardized methods to detail language skills if the test demonstrates areas of deficiency.

- Quantify correct and incorrect responses for a particular language skill.
- Devise a specific treatment goal based on information provided by the test.

Follow the progress of the treatment based on targeted language skill goals.

Practice Test

Practice Questions

1.   Which theory/theories of language acquisition emphasize(s) nature over **nurture?**
a. Relational frame theory
b. Generativist theories
c. Social interactionism
d. Emergentist theories
e. Empiricist theories

2.   Which of the following is not a part of Chomsky's transformational grammar?
a. Deep structure
b. Structural changes
c. Surface structure
d. Hidden assumptions
e. All of these are parts

3.   MacWhinney's Competition Model is a language development theory that is:
a. Emergentist
b. Empiricist
c. Behavioral
d. Nativist
e. None of these

4.   Since the 1980s, linguists and psychologists influenced by Piaget:
a. Have found interaction of nature and nurture as important
b. Have found the role of inherent structures more important
c. Have found the role of learning processes more important
d. Have found all of these to be equally important.
e. Have found none of these to be as important as other factors.

5.   At approximately what age do children begin to give names to things?
a. Between birth and four months of age
b. Between four and six months of age
c. Between six months and one year old
d. Between one year and eighteen months
e. Between eighteen and 24 months of age

6.   Which of the following observations does not support Chomsky's theory?
a. Children learn from experience the probability that one word will follow another.
b. Children in different countries go through similar stages of language development.
c. Children overregularize irregular verbs without having heard any examples of this.
d. Children learn correct syntax in spite of parents' inconsistency in correcting them.
e. Children invent unique languages in the absence of exposure to standard language.

7. A unit of sound is a:
   a. Morpheme
   b. Grapheme
   c. Phoneme
   d. Chereme
   e. Lexeme

8. The International Phonetic Alphabet symbol /ʌ/ corresponds to:
   a. The vowel sound in "book"
   b. The vowel sound in "buck"
   c. The vowel sound in "back"
   d. The vowel sound in "beak"
   e. The vowel sound in "beck"

9. The International Phonetic Alphabet symbol / ʃ / represents the initial consonant sound in:
   a. "Sass"
   b. "Foe"
   c. "The"
   d. "She"
   e. "Cha"

10. People in the southern United States tend to pronounce the words "pin" and "pen" the same way while people in the northern United States do not because:
    a. Historically Southerners could not spell.
    b. Nasality obscures similar vowel sounds.
    c. Southern speech has fewer vowel sounds.
    d. Southerners don't know word meanings.
    e. Of homophony with nasality in some dialects

11. Mary Ellen has diagnoses of cerebral palsy and spastic dysarthria. The second one means:
    a. She cannot hear speech.
    b. She cannot hear anything.
    c. She cannot produce speech.
    d. She cannot understand words.
    e. She cannot sort speech sounds.

12. The study of sentence structure and word order is called:
    a. Syntax
    b. Semantics
    c. Pragmatics
    d. Morphology
    e. None of these

13. The late great linguist Raven McDavid used to love to tell a story about a Southerner in a Northern restaurant who found his glass of water was not cold enough and asked the waitress for "a piece of ice." When McDavid told this story using a Southern dialect to a class of graduate students, much merriment ensued. McDavid's story was an illustration of:
    a. Regional differences in vocabulary
    b. Regional differences in pronunciation
    c. Regional differences in word meaning
    d. Regional differences in slang expressions
    e. Regional differences in the way ice is used

14. In the United States, making a circle with thumb and finger(s) means "okay." Which of the following is true about this gesture in other countries?
    a. In France this signifies "money."
    b. In Japan it is an obscene gesture.
    c. In Brazil this represents "zero."
    d. In Germany it means "worthless."
    e. None of these statements is true.

15. Where is it not an insult to sit with the soles of your shoes visible?
    a. Japan
    b. France
    c. Thailand
    d. Venezuela
    e. Middle East

16. A child in which of the following places is most likely to be offended by being patted on the head?
    a. Asia
    b. Poland
    c. Russia
    d. Argentina
    e. Czechoslovakia

17. While the anatomy and physiology of speech production is more than the sum of its parts, for the sake of convenience the speech mechanism can be divided into four phases. Which of the following is not one of these?
    a. Respiration
    b. Phonation
    c. Modulation
    d. Articulation
    e. Resonance

18. The parts of the body associated most closely with speech production obviously include the oral cavity, including the lips, tongue, and teeth. Which of the following is not one of the body parts *normally* most closely involved?
   a. The lungs
   b. The larynx
   c. The trachea
   d. The esophagus
   e. The nasal cavities

19. Which extrinsic muscle of the larynx is not a suprahyoid muscle?
   a. The digastric muscle
   b. The stylohyoid muscle
   c. The mylohyoid muscle
   d. The geniohyoid muscle
   e. The sternohyoid muscle

20. Which of these theories of voice production was not first proposed in the 19th century?
   a. Myoelastic-aerodynamic theory
   b. Neurochronoaxic theory
   c. Cavity-tone theory
   d. Harmonic theory
   e. These all were

21. Of the five senses, which one's input reaches the cerebral cortex without going through the thalamus?
   a. Vision
   b. Hearing
   c. Gustation
   d. Olfaction
   e. Touch/pain

22. How many cranial nerves are there in the human central nervous system?
   a. Eight
   b. Ten
   c. Twelve
   d. Six
   e. Fourteen

23. Of the cranial nerves, which have sensory, not motor functions?
   a. Olfactory
   b. Optic
   c. Auditory
   d. All these
   e. None of these

24. Of the cranial nerves, which have motor, not sensory functions?
    a. Trochlear
    b. Abducent
    c. Accessory
    d. Hypoglossal
    e. All of these

25. Which cranial nerves have both sensory and motor functions?
    a. Trigeminal
    b. Facial
    c. Vagus
    d. Glossopharyngeal
    e. All of these

26. Echolalia is:
    a. Repeating oneself over and over
    b. Repeating what other people say
    c. Hearing echoes of others' speech
    d. Only experienced by the autistic
    e. Only experienced by the retarded

27. Marco's first language is Castilian Spanish. His English is fluent, but his teacher refers him to the speech-language pathologist for what she calls a "lisp." Upon testing it is found that this feature of his articulation is systematically used only in words with the letter "c" followed by a vowel. The most likely explanation is:
    a. Marco's first language is influencing his second language.
    b. Marco is demonstrating a systematic articulation disorder.
    c. Marco's ESL status is combining with an articulation error.
    d. None of these is a likely explanation for what is described.
    e. All of these are equally likely to explain what is described.

28. Jason is a bright, happy, active four-year-old whose IQ scores are above average. He is healthy and his audiological testing is normal. His mother reports that 2-3 days after birth he was observed to have jaundice and lethargy, which resolved in an equally short time. These symptoms were recorded at the hospital but not diagnosed or treated as they resolved so quickly. Jason is referred to SLP because his speech is fluent but characterized by substitution of glottal stops for many consonants, which he seems unable to produce by using the normal configurations of tongue, teeth, and shape of the oral cavity. The most likely reason for this is that:
    a. Jason is simply lazy about using his mouth and is using his throat instead.
    b. Jason's development is normal; his speech will correct without treatment.
    c. Jason formed this habit in his early speech and just did not grow out of it.
    d. Jason does not pronounce many consonants right as he cannot hear them.
    e. Jason probably sustained minimal neurological damage when a newborn.

29. When you make the sounds /t/, /d/, /s/, or /z/, normally your tongue is in contact with:
    a. Your upper teeth.
    b. Your alveolar ridge.
    c. Your lower teeth.
    d. Your soft palate.
    e. Your hard palate.

30. Arlene was born blind and deaf. Which maternal condition was most likely to have caused this?
    a. Her mother had contracted rubella while in her first trimester.
    b. Her mother ate fish contaminated by mercury while pregnant.
    c. Her mother was smoking cigarettes throughout her pregnancy.
    d. Her mother regularly drank alcohol throughout her pregnancy.
    e. Her mother frequently abused cocaine while she was pregnant.

31. Jane is a native speaker of American English. She is seven years old. She is lisping this year whereas she was not doing so last year. Why is this likely?
    a. She lost all of her front baby teeth this year.
    b. She picked up a bad habit from her friends.
    c. It is a late-developing articulation disorder.
    d. She is reacting to social or academic stress.
    e. Her vocabulary has grown and contains words that are more difficult to pronounce.

32. Tommy is diagnosed with Broca's aphasia. What is not true related to this diagnosis?
    a. The source of the problem is damage to part of his brain.
    b. Tommy probably has trouble with spoken word retrieval.
    c. Tommy should be able to understand what is said to him.
    d. Expressive and receptive language are equally impacted.
    e. This is a neurological and language problem, rather than a speech problem.

33. Clara has a diagnosis of Wernicke's aphasia. What is not true about this disorder?
    a. Clara can speak fluently but cannot understand what others say.
    b. Clara's speech makes sense but will deteriorate without feedback.
    c. Clara's words all have meaning but are not arranged in proper order.
    d. Clara will probably develop compensatory strategies like stock phrases.
    e. Clara's disorder is caused by damage sustained in certain brain regions.

34. Children found to have learning disabilities related to language are most likely to have problems with:
    a. Morphology
    b. Syntax
    c. Semantics
    d. Memory
    e. All of these

35. Which of these instruments tests both receptive and expressive language?
    a. The TACL
    b. The ACLC
    c. The NSST
    d. Peabody
    e. All these

36. Which test assesses knowledge of the meaning of English and Spanish words?
    a. TOLD: Picture Vocabulary subtest
    b. Peabody Picture Vocabulary Test
    c. Toronto Tests of Receptive Vocabulary
    d. None of these includes Spanish words.
    e. All of these incorporate Spanish words.

37. Which of these semantic intervention tasks is most similar to Sentence Completion?
    a. Cloze format
    b. Using riddles
    c. 20 Questions
    d. Role playing
    e. None of these

38. Which of these intervention formats would be least applicable to learning synonyms and antonyms?
    a. Identification, differentiation, and elaboration of meaning
    b. Semantic classification and categorization
    c. Judgment of consistency of meaning
    d. Lexical paraphrasing
    e. All of these would be equally applicable

39. What is not a characteristic or tendency that would cause difficulty with semantics?
    a. Concrete thinking
    b. Literal thinking
    c. Limited imagery
    d. Divergent thinking
    e. Narrow perception

40. Which test does not assess immediate recall of digit series *both* forward and backward?
    a. McCarthy Scales: Numerical Memory
    b. ITPA: Auditory Sequential subtest
    c. WISC-IV: Digit Span subtest
    d. None of these assesses this
    e. All of these evaluate this

41. In audiology, what does MCL stand for?
    a. Maximum Comfort Level
    b. Minimum Clarity Locutions
    c. Medial Collateral Ligaments
    d. Media Convergence Lab
    e. Most Comfortable Loudness

42. A "notch" audiogram (sometimes called "cookie-bite") with a sharp dip in acuity around 4,000 Hz typically represents what kind of hearing?
    a. A normal curve of hearing
    b. Noise-induced hearing loss
    c. Conductive hearing losses
    d. Age-related hearing losses
    e. It represents none of these.

43. Which of the following is not one of the ossicles?
    a. The stapedius
    b. The stapes
    c. The malleus
    d. The incus
    e. They all are

44. What would not cause a conductive hearing loss?
    a. Obstruction by a foreign body in the ear
    b. Perforation of the tympanic membrane
    c. Exposure to excessively loud noises
    d. Damage to one or more ossicles
    e. All of these could cause a conductive hearing loss.

45. What is not a source of sensorineural hearing loss?
    a. Destruction of hair cells in the cochlea
    b. Damage to one or more of the ossicles
    c. Exposure to excessively loud noises
    d. A common progression of old age
    e. None of these is a source of sensorineural hearing loss.

46. Békésy audiometry differs from standard audiometry by:
    a. Testing many more frequencies than usual
    b. Allowing subjects to test their own hearing
    c. Continuous, not discrete, intensity changes
    d. Doing choices (b) and (c) but not choice (a)
    e. Doing all of these – choices (a), (b), and (c)

47. In audiology, what is UCL?
    a. Ultimate comfortable level
    b. Usual communication losses
    c. Uncomfortable loudness level
    d. Upper confidence limit (or level)
    e. Universal communications language

48. What does recruitment mean in audiology?
    a. Reduced range between threshold, MCL, and UCL
    b. Recruiting other nerves to supplant damaged nerves
    c. Recruiting hearing acuity for barely audible sounds
    d. Recruiting others to help in absence of a hearing aid

e. Abnormally wide range between threshold and MCL

49. Antoine is a second-grader whom Glenda the SLP is evaluating at the beginning of the school year. His IQ and achievement tests are below average, but not profoundly so. When she tests his hearing, he initially responds normally, following the directions to raise his left or right hand when he hears a tone in his left or right ear. But after a couple of minutes he stops responding. Glenda keeps increasing the intensity of the tones but still gets no response. She tests the machine again by listening to the earphones herself and they work. She can get Antoine's attention easily by tapping him on the shoulder, standing in front of him, or talking to him, and he understands and answers questions. Even stranger, his teacher also reports he seems to hear and understand what is said to him. Glenda runs into her predecessor in the SLP position, who was promoted and still visits the school as part of her new job. She reports having the exact same experience with Antoine last year. So does the audiologist when she makes her periodic visit. While the school team will need neurological/psychological/psychiatric consultations for this phenomenon, which of the following is the most likely explanation for it?
    a. Antoine is faking a hearing loss to receive special education or attention.
    b. Antoine is suffering from conversion hysteria or psychogenic deafness.
    c. Antoine is demonstrating the classic symptoms of organic hearing loss.
    d. Antoine is likely to have some attentional or neurological deficiencies.
    e. Antoine is most likely not experiencing any of these situations.

50. Presbycusis is most often characterized by:
    a. More loss at lower frequencies
    b. More loss at middle frequencies
    c. Uniform loss at all frequencies
    d. No particular frequency pattern
    e. More loss at higher frequencies

51. Dysarthria is:
    a. A neurologically caused articulation disorder
    b. A learning disability affecting reading ability
    c. A neurologically caused swallowing disorder
    d. An articulation disorder of the speech organs
    e. Speech defects related to mental impairment

52. Which of the following malocclusions is *most* likely to cause distortion of sibilants?
    a. Overbite
    b. Open-bite
    c. Underbite
    d. Cross-bite
    e. Collapsed bite

53. Willie is a man in his 50s who sustained brain damage due to head injuries from multiple motor vehicle accidents. He now has motor apraxia. This means that:
    a. When he walks, he appears to be drunk.
    b. He can use his upper but not lower body.
    c. He is paralyzed in both the upper and lower parts of his body.
    d. He cannot control external speech organs.

e. He can speak but not understand speech.

54. Mrs. Stokes is an elderly woman who suffered a cerebrovascular stroke. She now has difficulty swallowing solid foods. She is most likely to have a diagnosis of:
    a. An esophageal dysphagia
    b. A functional dysphagia
    c. Oropharyngeal dysphagia
    d. An esophageal achalasia
    e. A case of odynophagia

55. Therapy for dysphagia includes all but which of these?
    a. Lip exercises
    b. Tongue exercises
    c. Jaw exercises
    d. Swallowing exercises
    e. All these are included

56. Among exercises to improve swallowing ability in cases of dysphagia, not all involve actually swallowing. One of these is the Shaker exercise, which involves lifting the head but not the shoulders while lying flat on the back. Which of the following is another swallowing exercise that does not involve swallowing?
    a. The Mendelsohn maneuver
    b. The hyoid lift maneuver
    c. The effortful swallow
    d. The supraglottic swallow
    e. The super supraglottic swallow maneuver

57. In Piaget's stage theory of cognitive development, which of the following is not a stage?
    a. Sensorineural
    b. Sensorimotor
    c. Preoperational
    d. Concrete operations
    e. Formal operations

58. What did the psychologist Lev Vygotsky mean by "private speech?"
    a. Talking to oneself as a pathological symptom
    b. Talking privately between two close friends
    c. Talking to oneself to direct one's behavior
    d. Talking privately among several intimates
    e. Talking about private, not public, subjects

59. What have researchers found about the language development of babies who watch "brain stimulation" videos designed for infants?
    a. These children tend to learn new words more rapidly than those not watching videos.
    b. These children learn words at the same rate as children whose parents read to them.
    c. These children learn words at the same rate whether parents discuss the videos or not.
    d. These children actually learn words faster than children whose parents read to them.
    e. These children learn words slower than if parents read to them or discuss the videos.

60. On which of the following does learning theory focus?
    a. Unconscious impulses
    b. Internal mechanisms
    c. Social relationships
    d. Observable behaviors
    e. It focuses on all these

61. Which of these techniques does systematic desensitization use?
    a. Exposure to excessive amounts of the stimulus found aversive
    b. Successive approximations of exposure to an aversive stimulus
    c. Extinction of the undesirable response to the aversive stimulus
    d. These are all techniques used in systematic desensitization
    e. None of these is a technique used in systematic desensitization

62. Wendy is a five-year-old who substitutes /w/ for /r/ in her speech. She is referred to
    you, the speech-language pathologist for her school, because her mother and her
    teacher are concerned about her articulation. Of the following things you could tell
    them, which would be correct?
    a. Wendy has an articulation disorder and must have speech therapy.
    b. Wendy has an idiolectal pronunciation that is unusual but normal.
    c. Wendy must have hearing loss, as /r/ is most often affected by it.
    d. Wendy is normal as the norm for correct /r/ production is 8 years.
    e. None of these would be a correct thing to tell them about Wendy.

63. Elise is a fourth-grader who palatalizes her /tʃ/sound (i.e. her tongue is pressed up
    against her hard palate), noticeably distorting it. Glenda the SLP mentions this student
    to her predecessor Linda, who was Elise's SLP last year, and Linda affirms she was
    completely unsuccessful in remediating this articulation error. Glenda hits upon the idea
    of giving Elise a tongue depressor, instructing her to use it initially to keep her tongue
    from touching her palate while producing the target phoneme. Once Elise has become
    accustomed to the feeling of this tongue position and the sound she produces, Glenda
    has her phase out the tongue depressor until eventually she is pronouncing the sound
    correctly without it. Which of the following conclusions about this episode is most
    likely?
    a. Elise's success this year is due to maturation alone and the treatment was
       superfluous.
    b. Glenda's solution of the tongue depressor was entirely responsible for Elise's success.
    c. Elise's success is most likely due to a combination of the therapy and her maturation.
    d. Elise's success was due to her choice to change her speech, not therapy or maturation.
    e. It is most likely that Elise's correction was sheer luck, not intervention or maturation.

64. In 1960, Glenda was seven and in third grade. Her teacher loudly corrected her in front of the whole class, exclaiming, "It's not 'toonip,' it's turnip! You don't pronounce your r's!" She sent Glenda to the school psychologist, who gave Glenda tests and concluded she was very bright but had a speech impediment. Glenda was upset, and spent recess alone repeatedly voicing "rrrrrr" aloud. Within a short time she had corrected her pronunciation. Which statement is most correct about this incident?
   a. Glenda's age, IQ, and motivation aided her self-correction, but she did not have a speech impediment.
   b. Glenda did have an articulation disorder, but her high IQ allowed her to self-correct it without a therapist.
   c. Glenda was past the age when she should have correct /r/ articulation and needed the push of the insult.
   d. Glenda was willful, deliberately chose to distort her /r/s, and only changed them to show the adults.
   e. None of these statements is a correct conclusion with regard to this incident about Glenda's speech.

65. Which is the most common form of stuttering?
   a. Neurogenic stuttering
   b. Psychogenic stuttering
   c. Developmental stuttering
   d. Both (b) and (c) are
   e. All are equally common

66. Stuttering involves disorders with which of these?
   a. Rate
   b. Rhythm
   c. Fluency
   d. None of these
   e. All of these

67. Which of the following is not true about stuttering?
   a. Approximately 3 million Americans stutter.
   b. Stuttering happens in individuals of all ages.
   c. It is most frequent between the ages of 2-5.
   d. In children it always lasts for several years.
   e. About 5% of children stutter at some point.

68. Which of these statements is not true of stuttering?
   a. Boys are twice as likely to stutter as girls are.
   b. As they age, fewer boys are likely to stutter.
   c. The majority of children outgrow stuttering.
   d. Around 1% or fewer of adults are stutterers.
   e. All of these statements are true of stuttering.

69. What is true regarding recent stuttering research findings?
    a. Three genes causing stuttering have now been isolated.
    b. One gene related to stuttering has now been identified.
    c. Developmental stuttering is not found to run in families.
    d. Familial stuttering is attributed to environmental factors.
    e. None of these is true regarding recent research findings.

70. Which of the following may be used in stuttering therapy?
    a. Training in stuttering modification
    b. Teaching fluency shaping behaviors
    c. Changing secondary covert aspects
    d. None of these is likely to be used
    e. All of these can be used in therapy

71. In Starkweather's (1987) demands/capacity model of stuttering, what is not true?
    a. Some individuals have a predisposition for their speech to break down.
    b. When demands exceed capacity, speech breaks down into dysfluency.
    c. Stressors in the social environment do not influence speech demands.
    d. Most stutterers report that their speech is "just fine" a lot of the time.
    e. All of these are true statements in Starkweather's stuttering model.

72. Which of these are not overt or core features of stuttering?
    a. Blocks
    b. Tremors
    c. Repetitions
    d. Avoidances
    e. Prolongations

73. People who stutter often have no trouble reciting poetry or singing. What is/are the best explanation(s) for this?
    a. The rate, rhythm, and pitch of their vocal output are predetermined for them.
    b. Propositional speech is more stressful for speakers than words given to them.
    c. The enjoyment found in reciting poetry or singing a song overrides the stutter.
    d. None of these choices is a good explanation for why this phenomenon occurs.
    e. Answer (a) is only true for singing; answer (b) is true with poetry and singing.

74. "When reading aloud, John will raise his hand to signal 90% of his stuttering occurrences without cueing." This is an example of a behavioral objective for:
    a. Speech awareness
    b. Speech description
    c. Speech modification
    d. Speech preparation
    e. None of these

75. "John will identify three physical signs of his anxiety right before introducing himself to a group." This is an example of a behavioral objective for:
    a. Emotional exploration
    b. Emotional awareness
    c. Emotional modification
    d. Emotional understanding
    e. None of these is correct

76. "He bad." "Where was you?" "That Renee toy." "She don't drive." "I knowed that." These expressions are most likely attributed to:
    a. Delayed language development
    b. Disorders of articulation
    c. Non-standard English
    d. None of these
    e. All of these

77. Which of the following is not a component of a lesson plan for speech-language therapy?
    a. Goals for the semester
    b. Behavioral objectives
    c. Describing activities
    d. Materials to be used
    e. All of these are parts

78. What have researchers found regarding articulation with cleft lip and cleft palate?
    a. Those with cleft lip only have basically normal articulation.
    b. Differences in repaired and unrepaired clefts are very large.
    c. Unilateral clefts allow better articulation than bilateral ones.
    d. Articulation is better with incomplete than complete clefts.
    e. Researchers have found all of these with cleft lip or palate.

79. Research has found which of the following types of consonants to have the highest rates of correct production in people with cleft palates?
    a. Nasal consonants
    b. Consonant glides
    c. Plosive stops
    d. Affricates
    e. Fricatives

80. Who of the following speech-language pathologists is/was not a specialist in the field of stuttering?
    a. George H. Shames
    b. Charles G. Van Riper
    c. Martin F. Schwartz
    d. Daniel R. Boone
    e. Gary J. Rentschler

81. Which of the following conditions affecting the voice is not responsive to voice therapy?
    a. Thickening of vocal cords
    b. Vocal nodules or polyps
    c. Laryngeal contact ulcers
    d. Acute infectious laryngitis
    e. These all respond to therapy

82. In addition to the conditions named in #81, which of these can cause voice disorders?
    a. Laryngeal papilloma
    b. Laryngeal carcinoma
    c. Changes of puberty
    d. Endocrine changes
    e. All of these can/do

83. Which is the least common feature of functional dysphonias?
    a. Breathy voice
    b. Hoarse voice
    c. Loud voice
    d. Weak voice
    e. Harsh voice

84. Of the following voice disorders, which is *most* likely to result in no voice at all?
    a. Spastic dysphonia
    b. Functional aphonia
    c. Vocal cord paralysis
    d. Ventricular dysphonia
    e. Laryngeal web/synechia

85. What is not a variable typically rated in a voice screening for school children?
    a. Rate
    b. Pitch
    c. Quality
    d. Loudness
    e. Resonance

86. Cleft palate is known to cause hypernasality. Among other organic etiologies, which does not cause a hypernasal voice?
    a. A short palate
    b. Surgical trauma
    c. Soft palate injury
    d. Neurological impairment
    e. All of these can cause it.

87. Who of the following will not benefit from voice therapy to reduce hypernasality?
    a. Patients who have had surgical or dental treatment
    b. Patients whose hypernasality is the functional kind
    c. Patients with structural velopharyngeal inadequacy
    d. Patients of all of these types would benefit from it
    e. Patients of none of these types will benefit from it

88. Of the following approaches, which is for treating hypernasality but not denasality?
    f. Feedback
    g. Ear training
    h. Target voice models
    i. Establishing new pitch
    j. Explanation of problem

89. What is not true about nasal emission?
    a. It is a type of nasal resonance problem.
    b. It can often accompany hypernasality.
    c. It can be due to palatal insufficiency.
    d. It rarely exists for functional reasons.
    e. It is not remediable by therapy alone.

90. Which is not a characteristic of voice differences in the deaf?
    a. Overly high pitch after puberty
    b. Overly high pitches at all ages
    c. Pharyngeal focus of resonance
    d. Severe denasality of the voice
    e. True hypernasality with some

91. Which of these is a prosthesis for voice production by laryngectomies?
    a. Blom-Singer
    b. VoiceMaster
    c. The ProVox
    d. None of these
    e. All of these

92. Which of these is not an electromechanical voice device for laryngectomy patients?
    a. The Servox
    b. Cooper-Rand
    c. Blom-Singer
    d. All of these
    e. None of these

93. What is not an advantage of electrolarynx devices?
    a. The quality of the voice tone produced
    b. Their use is quickly and easily learned
    c. They are able to produce a loud voice
    d. No interference with other methods
    e. These are relatively less expensive

94. What is not a disadvantage of electrolarynx devices?
    a. Fibrosis limits transmission
    b. Manual dexterity is needed
    c. The conspicuous appearance
    d. Loudness of the voice tone
    e. The sound of the voice tone

95. After total laryngectomy, some patients may use a device called HME. This is:
    a. Used to prosthetically produce a voice tone
    b. Used to protect the airway with respiration
    c. Used to electromechanically produce voice
    d. Used to perform none of these functions
    e. Used to perform all of these functions

96. With the tracheoesophageal puncture technique and silicone prosthesis insertion, what is not an advantage?
    a. The quality of the voice tone produced
    b. The high success rates of usable voice
    c. The minimal teaching that is required
    d. None of these is an advantage of TEP.
    e. All of these are advantages with TEP.

97. What is not a disadvantage of silicone prostheses inserted via the tracheoesophageal puncture (TEP) technique for a postoperative total laryngectomy patient?
    a. Daily maintenance of the prosthesis
    b. Recurrent leakage after time passes
    c. Periodic need to replace the device
    d. Low resistance to the flow of air
    e. The expenses associated with it

98. Today, which is not one of the characteristics that good voice prostheses should have?
    a. Safe and reliable use
    b. Frontloading insertion
    c. Enlargement of fistula
    d. Low airflow resistance
    e. Semipermanent fixation

Answer Key

1. b	11. c	21. d	31. a	41. e	51. a	61. b	71. c	81. d	91. e
2. e	12. a	22. c	32. d	42. b	52. b	62. d	72. d	82. e	92. c
3. a	13. b	23. d	33. c	43. a	53. d	63. c	73. e	83. c	93. a
4. c	14. e	24. e	34. e	44. c	54. c	64. a	74. a	84. b	94. d
5. d	15. d	25. c	35. b	45. b	55. e	65. c	75. b	85. a	95. b
6. a	16. a	26. b	36. c	46. d	56. b	66. e	76. c	86. e	96. e
7. c	17. c	27. a	37. a	47. c	57. a	67. d	77. e	87. c	97. d
8. b	18. d	28. e	38. b	48. a	58. c	68. b	78. b	88. d	98. c
9. d	19. e	29. b	39. d	49. d	59. e	69. a	79. a	89. a	
10. e	20. b	30. a	40. b	50. e	60. d	70. e	80. d	90. b	

Answers and Explanations

1. B: Generativist theories (b) of grammar such as those of Noam Chomsky and Eric Lenneberg emphasize nature over nurture. They posit the existence of innate abilities (nature) such as a language acquisition device as being more fundamental to language development than environmental influences (nurture). Relational frame theory (a) is based on operant conditioning and therefore emphasizes the role of the environment in language learning. Social interactionism (c), emergentist theories (d) and empiricist theories (e) of language development all focus more on the interactions between nature and nurture rather than emphasizing either one over the other.

2. E: All of these are parts (e) of Chomsky's transformational grammar. Deep structure (a) is what Chomsky said was the original form in which we conceive a linguistic expression, which often does not follow rules of grammar. Compliance with those rules involves structural changes (b) or transformations. Surface structure (c) is the expression following those transformations, which does observe grammatical rules. For example, a deep structure might be something like "me + go." The mind performs transformations to reflect the subject of a sentence rather than the object, and the tense of a verb, to produce a surface structure like "I went." Transformations also change statements into questions ("why you not go" becomes "why didn't you go?"), add "-'s" to make a proper noun possessive ("Tommy ball" becomes "Tommy's ball", etc. With the elements "John" + "kiss" + "Mary," two different surface structures such as "Mary kissed John" and "John was kissed by Mary" have the same deep structure and the same meaning. Hidden assumptions (d) or biases are knowledge that nativist theorists like Chomsky believe are inherent and allow children to ascertain rapidly what is/is not possible in their language's grammar, and to achieve mastery of the grammar by the age of three.

3. A: MacWhinney's Competition Model is an (a) emergentist theory of language development. Such theories claim that language acquisition is a cognitive process emerging from the interactions of biology and the environment. Empiricist (b) theories arose as a reaction against nativist theories which emphasized the innate nature of language acquisition. These include relational frame theory, social interactionist theory (see also #1), statistical learning theories, and functional linguistics. Empiricism recognizes the interaction between nature and nurture, but puts more emphasis on the role of learning, or nurture, and finds that the inherent, or nature, part is a general cognitive learning mechanism. Behavioral (d) theories such as Skinner's find language acquisition to be a form of operant conditioning in which linguistic behavior is shaped by the consequences of verbal responses. Nativist (d) theories include Chomsky's transformational grammar (see also #2) or generative grammar and the theories of Jerry Fodor and Eric Lenneberg. These theories view the acquisition of language as being based more on inherent abilities or mechanisms than on environmental influences. Since (a) is correct, answer (e), none of these, is incorrect.

4. C: Those influenced by Piaget's theory of cognitive development (c) have found the role of learning processes to be more important than previously thought. Piaget believed that children learn by interacting with and acting upon their environments, and that in so doing, they construct knowledge (constructivism). These beliefs are compatible with placing more importance on learning processes than on inherent structures (b), such as a language acquisition device (LAD) and a universal grammar, which are emphasized by nativist theories. While most theories recognize the interaction of nature and nurture (a) to some degree, those subscribing to Piaget's models have come to feel since the 1980s that learning processes play a more important role than previously realized. Social interactionist theory and emergentist theories place more emphasis on the interactions of both. Since (c) is correct, answer (d), all of these, and (e), none of these, are incorrect.

5. D: Children begin naming things (d) between the ages of one year and eighteen months, most commonly around the age of one year. Between birth and four months (a), infants cry and make cooing noises, and they attend to emotional tones and rhythms in speech they hear. Between four and six months (b), babies begin to distinguish the main vowel and consonant sounds of their native languages in speech they hear. Between six months and one year (c), children can recognize words within the flow of speech they hear. At seven months, a baby may recognize and remember individual words, but may not recognize the same word uttered by different speakers. By 10 months, a child can do this. In addition to naming things, children also begin to use symbolic gestures (e.g. shrugging to indicate "I don't know" or spreading the arms wide to indicate "big" or "a lot") at the end of the first year (d). Between 18 and 24 months (e), children start speaking in two- and three-word phrases, often called telegraphic speech, and can understand the meanings of verbs based on the contexts in which they are used.

6. A: The observation that (a) children learn the probability that one word will follow another from experience supports statistical learning theories of language development, not Chomsky's theory. In statistical learning theory, children experience the probability that one word will follow another, and generalize their learning to patterns and categories of word order. The observation that children with different languages go through similar developmental stages in learning language (b) supports Chomsky's theory of universal grammar. Overregularization of irregular verbs, such as "goed" or "taked," reflects a basic understanding of how regular verbs conjugate. Children applying the rule to irregular verbs without having heard such constructions supports Chomsky's theory of inherent linguistic structures. The observation that children eventually learn to create grammatically correct sentences even though their parents are not consistent in correcting them (d) supports Chomsky's theory and opposes behavioral theories, in that their learning is due to innate structures rather than to environmental experience. The observation that children may invent unique languages when not exposed to a standard language (e) supports Chomsky's theory of innate devices enabling language development. Researchers found a group of deaf children in Nicaragua who could not hear spoken Spanish and were never taught any standard sign language. These children invented their own sign language, which was grammatically complex and was not related to Spanish or to any standard sign language.

7. C: A phoneme (c) is a single unit of sound. A morpheme (a) is a unit of semantic meaning, which may be a word or a syllable (such as "un" or "-s"). A grapheme (b) is a unit of written language as opposed to spoken language. A chereme (d) is the sign-language equivalent of a spoken-language phoneme, i.e. a single unit of gestural language. A lexeme (e) is unit of morphological analysis; unlike the other choices, it is abstract. It represents a set of the forms a word, such as a verb, can take. For the forms "to run, run, ran, runs, running," the lexeme is "run." Lexemes make up a lexicon; these words come from the same root. With the exception of lexemes, the other "-emes" listed here refer to the smallest identifiable unit, of sound or of meaning.

8. B: The symbol /ʌ/ corresponds to the sound in "buck" (b). The sound in "book" (a) is represented by the symbol /ʊ/. The sound in "back" (c) is denoted by the symbol /æ/ (called "ash"). The sound in "beak" (d) is shown by the symbol /i/, which is the letter used in Latin, Latinate (Romance) and other languages to represent this sound, usually spelled in English words with "e," "ee," "ea," "ei," or "ie." The sound in "beck" (e) is represented phonetically by the symbol /ɛ/.

9. D: The symbol /ʃ/ represents the first sound in (d) "She," the "sh" sound. The "s" sound in "sass" (a) is /s/ in the International Phonetic Alphabet. The "f" sound in "fist" (b) is also /f/. The vocalized "th" sound in "the" (c) is shown with the symbol /ð/. The sound in "cha" (e) as in "cha-cha" is actually a combination of a /t/ sound and the /ʃ/ sound in "she" (d). As such it is represented by the symbol /tʃ/.

10. E: The "pin"/"pen" phenomenon is an example of (e) homophony in a nasal environment which occurs in some dialects, such as Southern American English. The nasality of the /n/ following the vowel in both words causes the vowels to sound the same in this regional dialect. This is not because Southerners historically couldn't spell (a). Spelling often has little to do with pronunciation, and the rich history of Southern literature further dispels the idea Southerners couldn't spell. The idea that the nasal /n/ sound obscures the distinction between /I/ and /ɛ/ (b) sounds plausible but is untrue. Southern speech does not have fewer vowel sounds (c) than Northern speech; many vowels are pronounced as diphthongs or triphthongs in the South, suggesting more vowel sounds. It is wholly untrue that Southerners do not know the meanings of these words (d), as evidenced by a common response in Southerners when hearing either word without sufficient context to distinguish the meaning; i.e. "Do you have a pen/pin?" will often be met with the response, "Do you mean an ink pen or a safety pin?" Linguists have demonstrated the homophony phenomenon with native Southerners by asking them to make a conscious effort to pronounce each vowel differently in isolation while nasalizing their speech; most cannot, producing the same vowel sound each time.

11. C: Spastic dysarthria means Mary Ellen (c) cannot produce speech sounds. She can vocalize but not verbalize. Her spasticity is a rigidity and incoordination of the muscles used to produce meaningful speech sounds due to damage to the parts of the brain that control these muscles. This term does not mean she is unable to hear speech (a). It does not mean she is deaf (b). It does not mean that she cannot understand words (d) or spoken language; this would be a definition of Wernicke's aphasia or receptive aphasia, a neurological disorder that interferes with processing receptive language. It does not

mean that she cannot sort or differentiate among speech sounds (e); she can understand what she hears but cannot reproduce it herself.

12. A: Sentence structure and word order and/or their study are called syntax (a). Semantics (b) refers to the study of meaning in language. Pragmatics (c) refers to the study of how context contributes to meaning. Morphology (d) refers to the study of the structure of words. Since (a) is correct, answer (e), none of these, is incorrect.

13. B: McDavid's story illustrated (b) regional differences in pronunciation. When he used a distinctive dialect from one of the Southern states, the word "ice," which Northerners are used to hearing phonetically as /ais/, sounded more like /æs/. Thus it sounded like "a piece of" something other than ice, explaining the students' hilarity (which was McDavid's intention). This did not illustrate regional differences in vocabulary (a) as the same word was used regardless of its pronunciation. It did not illustrate regional differences in word meaning (c) as the word "ice" means the same in the Northern and Southern U.S. It was rather that the hearer could *interpret* what the speaker said to be a different word with a different meaning, but this was due to his pronunciation rather than to any different meanings of the word he was actually saying. The story did not illustrate regional differences in slang expressions (d), as the Northerner unfamiliar with the Southern dialect who would misinterpret the word used by the Southerner would think he was using a slang expression which means the same thing in both North and South. The story did not illustrate regional differences in the way ice is used (e); both regions of the U.S. are familiar with adding ice to drinks.

14. E: None of these statements is true (e). This gesture does have different meanings in the countries named, but the meanings given are assigned to the wrong countries. In France the thumb/finger circle does not mean "money" (a); it means "zero" or "worthless." In Japan this gesture is not obscene (b); it means "money." In Brazil this gesture does not mean "zero" (c) as it does in France; it is an obscene gesture there. In Germany this gesture does not mean "worthless" (d) as it does in France; it is an obscene gesture in Germany as it is in Brazil.

15. D: It is not considered an insult in Venezuela (d) to sit with the soles of your shoes visible (as when you cross your legs). However, to do this in Japan (a), France (b), Thailand (c), Middle Eastern countries (e), and Near Eastern countries is considered insulting because you are showing the lowest and dirtiest part of your body to others, which these cultures find rude.

16. A: A child in Asia (a) is most likely to be offended by being patted on the head. In the Buddhist religion, the head is where the soul resides. So in cultures most influenced by Buddhism, children are likely to feel uncomfortable having their heads touched. Poland (b), Russia (c), Argentina (d), and Czechoslovakia (e) are not known for having as large numbers of Buddhists as countries in Asia are, so children in these countries are much less likely to be offended by head-patting for religious reasons. There are not other cultural traditions in these countries that would contribute to a similar aversion to having the head touched.

17. C: Modulation (c) is not one of the four phases of the speech mechanism. Modulation can mean varying the pitch, tone, or intensity of one's voice, which will determine the prosody of a person's speech, but is not one of the actual phases of producing speech. The phases are respiration (a) or breathing, which is required to provide a stream of air; phonation (b) or producing sound by using the air to vibrate the vocal folds and/or other parts of the vocal tract; articulation (d) or altering the specific qualities of phonation to produce various specific vowel and consonant sounds, mainly by changing the shape of the oral cavity as well as manipulating the tongue, teeth, lips to block or release airflow; and resonance (e) or the natural frequency of vibration of the vocal apparatus.

18. D: The esophagus (d) is not *normally* most closely involved in speech production. The exception is when a person has had a laryngectomy, i.e. the removal of the larynx, usually in cases of laryngeal cancer. In these cases, the individual cannot phonate normally. Such individuals often learn esophageal speech, wherein they swallow air and then burp, using their other speech production parts to shape this belched air into speech sounds. However, most individuals have intact larynxes and do not use esophageal speech. The body parts most closely involved are the lungs, larynx, trachea, and nasal cavities. The lungs (a) supply the necessary air stream. The larynx (b) is at the top of the trachea and creates a valve to open and close the air stream. It is used in producing speech and also in coughing, vomiting, urinating, moving the bowels, and heavy lifting. The trachea (c), commonly known as the windpipe, is vertically between the larynx and the bronchi and in front of the esophagus. It is made up of cartilage rings, fibrous tissue, and smooth muscle, giving it the flexibility to accommodate changes in air pressure within the chest. The nasal cavities (e) are involved in inhaling and exhaling air, producing nasal speech sounds, and contributing to resonance, as well as controlling temperature, humidity, and inhaled particles.

19. E: The sternohyoid muscle (e) is not a suprahyoid muscle but is an infrahyoid muscle. It originates in the sternum as its name implies, specifically in the manubrium sterni, and inserts on the hyoid bone. The digastric muscle (a) originates in its posterior at the mastoid process and inserts on the hyoid bone; its anterior originates in the hyoid bone and inserts on the mandible (lower jawbone). The stylohyoid (b) originates in the styloid process and inserts on the hyoid bone. The mylohyoid (c) is a sheet of muscle fibers forming the muscular floor of the mouth. Its fibers run along a bony ridge called the mylohyoid line on the inner surface of the mandible. The geniohyoid (d) muscle fibers originate via a short tendon in the lower mental spine at the mandibular symphysis and insert on the anterior surface of the hyoid bone. The suprahyoid muscles are all laryngeal elevators, i.e. they lift up the larynx. Infrahyoid muscles such as the sternohyoid (e) are, along with the omohyoid muscles, the "strap muscles" of the neck. The sternohyoid pulls the hyoid bone down, and keeps it fixated in place when the mandible is opened against resistant force.

20. B: Neurochronoaxic theory (b) was not first proposed in the 19th century. It was proposed by Raoul Husson in 1950 and is the only theory listed here that was formulated in the 20th century. The myoelastic-aerodynamic theory (a) was proposed by Johannes Müller in 1843 and has been very popular ever since. It states that the vocal folds are subject to well-known aerodynamic and physical principles. According to this theory, the frequency and mode of vibration of the vocal folds depend on their length related to tension and mass and their boundaries, and on the properties of mucus, mucous membranes, connective tissue, and muscle tissue, which properties in turn are regulated by the interaction of the laryngeal muscles. The cavity-tone theory (c) was proposed by Willis in 1830. In this theory, vowel sounds depended on the length of the resonating tube and were independent of the "reed" tone, based on the analogy with early "talking machines" consisting of an air supply, a reed, a resonator, and a cover. The harmonic theory (d), proposed by Charles Wheatstone in 1837, postulated that the reed tone described by Willis was not a pure tone but a complex tone with many harmonics or overtones and that vowel sounds resulted from augmentation of some harmonics. Accordingly the harmonic theory is also called the overtone theory or the steady state theory. As (b) was not first proposed in the 19th century, answer (e), these all were, is incorrect.

21. D: Olfaction (d) or the sense of smell is the only sense which does not make a synapse in the thalamus before proceeding to the cerebral cortex. Visual information (a) travels via the optic nerve to the superior colliculus, the thalamus, and the visual cortex in the occipital lobe at the rear of the cerebral cortex. Auditory information (b) travels from the cochlea via the auditory nerve to the inferior colliculus of the side of the midbrain opposite the hearing ear, then to the auditory cortex, to the cochlear branch of cranial nerve VIII (acoustic), to the cochlear nucleus of the brain's medulla. Gustatory information (c) travels via cranial nerves VII (facial nerve), IX (glossopharyngeal nerve) and X (vagus nerve) to the nucleus solitarius in the medulla and then to the gustatory cortex. Tactile sensations (e) are received by specialized neurons: thermoreceptors for temperature, tactile mechanoreceptors for touch, and nocireceptors for pain. All of these synapse in the cerebral cortex. In contrast, olfactory sensations (d) are received by olfactory receptor neurons which pass through the cribiform plate and make a synapse in the olfactory bulb. From the olfactory bulb the impulses go straight to the cerebral cortex. Olfactory centers are connected to structures that process memories and emotions such as the amygdala and hippocampus. This may explain why certain smells will trigger vivid, emotionally charged memories.

22. C: There are twelve (c) cranial nerves in the human CNS. They are: I – olfactory; II – optic; III – oculomotor; IV – trochlear; V – trigeminal; VI – abducent; VII – facial; VIII – auditory or acoustic; IX – glossopharyngeal; X – vagus; XI – accessory; and XII – hypoglossal. There are not eight (a), ten (b), six (d), or fourteen (e) cranial nerves, so these answers are all incorrect. A helpful mnemonic that many medical students use to remember these nerves is: "On Old Olympus' Towering Top, A Finn And German Viewed A Hop." The initial letters of each word correspond to the initial letters of each nerve.)

23. D: All these (d) have sensory functions. The olfactory (a) nerve, CN I, transmits sensory impulses of smell. The optic (b) nerve, CN II, transmits sensory impulses of vision. The auditory (c) nerve, CN VIII, transmits sensory impulses of hearing. Since (d) is correct, answer (e), none, is incorrect.

24. E: All of these (e) cranial nerves have motor functions. The trochlear (a) nerve, CN IV, controls the motors to rotate the eyes outward and downward. The abducent (b) nerve, CN VI, supplies the lateral eye muscles. The accessory (c) nerve, CN XI, innervates the muscles of the pharynx, larynx, soft palate, and neck. The hypoglossal (d) nerve, CN XII, supplies the strap muscles of the neck and the internal and external muscles of the tongue. Also, the oculomotor nerve, CN III, has the motor functions of visual convergence and accommodation, allowing binocular vision.

25. C: All of these (e) cranial nerves serve both sensory and motor functions. The trigeminal (a) nerve, CN V, transmits sensations in the eye, nose, and face and also innervates muscles of the tongue and muscles used in chewing. The facial (b) nerve, CN VII, transmits sensations in the tongue and soft palate and also innervates muscles in the face and the stapedius muscle, which connects to the stapes (stirrup) in the middle ear. The vagus (c) nerve, CN X, transmits sensations in the ears, pharynx, larynx, and viscera and also innervates muscles of the pharynx, larynx, tongue, and the viscera's smooth muscles. The glossopharyngeal (d) nerve, CN IX, transmits sensations in the tonsils, pharynx, and soft palate and also innervates muscles of the pharynx and stylopharyngeus.

26. B: Echolalia is (b) repeating what other people say. People who display this behavior may only repeat what others say exclusively and never make any original utterances of their own, or they may be able both to engage in purposeful speech at times and engage in repetition at times. Echolalia is not repeating oneself (a). It is not hearing echoes of speech (c). Echolalia is not experienced only by those with autistic disorders (d) or only by those with mental retardation (e). Both individuals with autism spectrum disorders and mental retardation may demonstrate echolalia. This is not a deliberate behavior meant to annoy others (though it can have that effect) but a symptom of neurological problems. Many people with autism have difficulties with social interactions, need rigid, circumscribed patterns of activity, and have an affinity for repetitive and mechanical actions; echolalia is a behavior that fits this profile. For some, it is the only way they can respond verbally to verbal stimuli from others. Echolalia, while seemingly meaningless in conversational and social terms, can be valuable as it demonstrates some limited ability to verbalize. Some therapists use echolalia as a starting point on which to build more functional verbal behavior.

27. A: The most likely explanation for this example is (a): Marco's first (native) language is influencing his second language. In Castilian, one dialect of Spanish, the letter "c" when followed by a vowel is not pronounced as /s/ as it is in English and in Catalan, South American, and other dialects of Spanish, but as /θ/ or theta, represented in the English alphabet as "th" (devocalized as in "thin" or "math," not vocalized as in "this" or "that"). With the similarities between Spanish and English, Marco is transferring his Spanish pronunciation to his English pronunciation. If the SLP does not find any physiological or possible neurological deficits in testing Marco, it is likely he is not showing a systematic articulation disorder (b) in which a person regularly mispronounces a certain phoneme or phonemes. If it is safe to assume he does not have an articulation disorder, then it follows that there is not such a disorder interacting with his ESL status (c). Since (a) is correct, answer (d), none of these, and (e), all of these, are both incorrect.

28. E: The most likely reason for Jason's substitution of glottal stops for many consonants normally shaped in the mouth with the aid of the tongue and teeth is that (e) the newborn's jaundice and lethargy were most likely symptoms of a virus which caused minimal neurological damage. This kind of damage can slightly impair specialized functions such as motor functions related to the oral apparatus. He may have sustained subtle damage to the glossopharyngeal nerve (CN IX), the vagus nerve (CN X), the accessory nerve (CN XI), and/or the hypoglossal nerve (CN XII) involved with the muscles of the pharynx, larynx, tongue, and soft palate. It is not likely that he is merely being lazy (a) as it is developmentally normal for a child to use the apparatus best suited to imitate the sounds he hears. The fact that Jason substitutes glottal stops for *many* consonants means it is not likely that this speech dysfunction will correct itself without treatment (b). Glottal stops are not features of many consonants in English, making Jason's substitution for many consonant sounds unusual. It is not likely that Jason simply formed a habit he did not grow out of (c) as making this substitution is not natural. He would be more likely to employ the usual oral structures. The glottal stops take more effort even though he is fluent. His speech is not caused by a hearing deficit (d); the example states that his audiological testing was normal.

29. B: The normal way a /t/ or /d/ is produced in English is by pressing the tip of the tongue against the alveolar ridge (b). In some American regional dialects, such as in working-class populations in areas of New York, Massachusetts or Connecticut, these sounds may be made with the tongue touching the upper teeth (a), but this is a dialect or what many people call an "accent." When pressing the tongue against the alveolar ridge, no other sounds but /t/ or /d/ are possible. (The only difference between the two is that /t/ is unvoiced while /d/ is voiced.) When the tongue is in close contact with the alveolar ridge but not pressed against it, allowing some air through, the unvoiced or voiced fricatives /s/ or /z/ are produced. It is impossible to produce these phonemes by pressing the tongue against the lower teeth (c). Pressing the back of the tongue against the place where the soft palate (d) meets the hard palate (e) produces the sounds /k/ or /g/ in the case of plosives, and by not pressing firmly produces /ʃ/ or /ʒ/ in the case of fricatives. (Affricates combine an alveolar stop with a fricative, such as /tʃ/ as in "cha-cha" or /dʒ/ as in "judge.")

30. A: The most likely cause for congenital blindness and deafness is maternal rubella (a) or German measles during pregnancy, especially in early pregnancy. Maternal mercury exposure via contaminated fish (b) is more likely (as is lead exposure) to cause lower IQ scores and attentional deficits in the infant than to cause blindness and deafness. Smoking cigarettes throughout pregnancy (c) is more likely to lead to miscarriages or abnormal fetal heartbeats, premature births, and low birth weights than to blindness and deafness. Drinking alcohol regularly while pregnant (d) is more likely to impair the child's attention span, IQ, cognitive abilities, and school achievement than to result in blindness and deafness. Moreover, consuming more than two drinks per day is likely to result in fetal alcohol syndrome, which includes low birth weight, reduced brain size, facial abnormalities, lack of motor coordination, and mental retardation, but not blindness and deafness. Use or abuse of cocaine (e) during pregnancy is more likely to cause smaller disruptions in the child's cognitive and linguistic abilities and larger problems with impulse control than to cause blindness and deafness.

31. A: The most likely reason Jane is lisping at seven when she did not at six is (a): she lost her front baby teeth this year. Without the barrier of the front teeth, fricatives like /s/ and /z/ easily become /θ/ or /ð/ as the tongue protrudes. It is unlikely that her friends were deliberately lisping and she joined in (b). It is unlikely to be a late-developing articulation disorder (c); articulation disorders producing lisps are more likely to develop as the child learns to speak. Absent any other physiological or psychological changes, an articulation disorder would not suddenly appear at age seven. A reaction to academic or social pressures (d) manifested in a speech disorder would more likely appear as stuttering. A child's growing vocabulary can cause mispronunciation of certain new words learned, but not of a specific phoneme she could already produce (e). Typically, children mispronounce words they have read but not heard, especially children who are advanced readers. This does not involve distorting or substituting "th" sounds for "s" or "z" sounds, but is more likely to involve omitting or adding sounds to the word, mispronouncing vowel sounds, putting stress on the wrong syllable, and similar errors.

32. D: What is not true is that (d) expressive and receptive language will be equally impacted. Broca's aphasia is thought to result from damage to Broca's area in the inferior frontal gyrus of the brain (a). New research suggests it may involve other areas as well. It is known for causing problems with expressive language more than with receptive language. Certain aspects of receptive language processing are affected in some patients, but these seem related to more difficult retrieval processes. It is common for those suffering from Broca's aphasia to have difficulty recalling words they want to use when speaking (b). Other aspects of spoken and written expression of language may be affected as well. Tommy should be able to understand what is said to him (c). There is a different type of aphasia (see #33), associated with damage to a different area of the brain, which interferes with receptive language. This is a neurological problem affecting language development and linguistic expression rather than a speech problem (e). Though difficulty with recalling words, arranging them in grammatical order, and other expressive language problems will certainly seem to disrupt the individual's speech, speech problems by definition disrupt the physical production of speech, whether they are neurological, physiological, or psychological in origin. For example, articulation disorders and stuttering are speech problems while aphasias and delayed language development are language problems.

33. C: It is not true that Clara's words are not arranged in proper order (c) though they are likely to have meaning. People with Wernicke's aphasia often speak fluently and with correct syntax. However, while they can express themselves in speech, their ability to process and understand the speech of others is significantly impaired (a). Therefore, though Clara's speech makes sense, eventually its meaning will break down due to the lack of feedback (b) from other people's speech which she cannot understand. Clara is likely to develop strategies, as most Wernicke's aphasia patients do, to compensate for and hide her lack of comprehension (d). For example, if asked "Where did you go yesterday?" and she cannot understand what you said, she may respond with something like, "Oh my, what a pretty dress you have on!" in an attempt to hide the fact that she doesn't know what you asked her, and to divert attention in the hope of having a successful social interaction. Clara's disorder is thought to be caused by damage to Wernicke's area (e), in the posterior of the superior temporal gyrus in the cerebral cortex, around the auditory cortex, on the Sylvian fissure where the temporal and parietal lobes of the brain meet. New research suggests that functions traditionally attributed to Wernicke's area take place more widely in the temporal and frontal lobes as well.

34. E: Children found to have learning disabilities related to language are likely to have problems with all of these (e). Delayed and disordered language development are more likely to present with global difficulties than isolated specific ones. Problems with morphology (a) will appear as difficulty with forming words. Problems with syntax (b) will be manifested in difficulty with forming sentences. Problems with semantics (c) will be seen by difficulty with understanding words and word relationships. Problems with memory (d) will be evidenced by difficulty with retention, such as remembering spoken messages, and retrieval, such as word finding, fluency, and speech flexibility. Fluency is shown by having words, phrases, and sentences readily available. Flexibility is demonstrated as ability to shift from one set of words, phrases, and sentences to another set or type, either adaptively in response to external changes or limits, or spontaneously. Other criteria for assessing language ability include creativity and elaboration.

35. B: The NSST (c) or Northwestern Syntax Screening Test has two sections, Receptive and Expressive. The TACL (a), or Test for Auditory Comprehension of Language, contains sections on Vocabulary, Morphology, and Syntax, but only tests the receptive side of language. Its format requires a child to point to one of several pictures that best illustrates the meaning of the word, phrase, or sentence spoken by the tester. The ACLC (b), or Assessment of Children's Language Comprehension, also assesses basic receptive language skills. It includes a section of vocabulary words and three sections of syntactic sequences (phrases or sentences). It also requires the child to point to the correct choice among several. The Peabody (d) Picture Vocabulary also asks the child to point to one of several pictures to identify which word (or occasional short phrase) the examiner speaks. Since only (c) is correct, answer (e), all these, is incorrect.

36. C: The Toronto Tests of Receptive Vocabulary (c), or TTRV, test knowledge of word meaning with both English and Spanish words. These tests contain an equal number of words (40) in each language. English and Spanish word choices are not identical. The Picture Vocabulary subtest of the TOLD (a), or Test of Language Development, does not include Spanish words. Neither does the Peabody Picture Vocabulary Test (b), or PPVT. These other tests only use English words. Since only (c) is correct, answer (e), all of these, is incorrect.

37. A: The semantic intervention most similar to Sentence Completion is the cloze format (a). This format can be oral or written. The only difference is that the missing word the child must supply can be in any part of the sentence, while in Sentence Completion the missing word is always at the end of the sentence. Therefore Sentence Completion is better for learning semantic rules for choosing words, relationships, or concepts that come at the end of a phrase or sentence, while cloze has a wider range of application. Examples of sentence completion using prototypical contexts are "I take my coat ___ (off/on/over); I put my shoes ___ (in/on/over)." Examples of sentence completion using verbal analogies are "Trees have leaves and birds have _____ (feathers); John is my uncle and Mary is my ___ (aunt); you drive a car and you fly a ___ (plane)." Cloze may use a paragraph in which certain parts of speech such as prepositions, as used in the first sentence completion example, are left blank throughout: "Billy has a green rug _ on the floor _ his room. There is a poster of a tiger _ the wall ___ his bed and a desk ___ to the window. He has an aquarium ___ fish _ them." Riddles (b) are good for teaching the consolidation of labels or names of things, animals, or people, i.e. teaching referential vocabulary. 20 Questions (c) is good for teaching verbal specificity by narrowing down groups of words according to their semantic class or to their shared features of meaning. Role playing (d) is good for teaching appropriate word, phrase, or sentence choices according to the social context. Since (a) is correct, answer (e), none of these, is incorrect.

38. B: Semantic classification and categorization (b) would be least applicable to learning synonyms and antonyms. This format is for classifying and categorizing objects, events, or words illustrated in pictures, and for identifying the semantic class to which they belong. Identification, differentiation, and elaboration of meaning (a) is for identifying similarities and differences in word meanings, so it is good for learning antonyms and synonyms. Judgment of consistency of meaning (c) is for identifying words, phrases, or clauses that violate the context (e.g. "The girl washed *itself.* Does this sentence make sense? Can you correct this?" or "The cat was sitting *in* the table. Does this make sense? Can you correct it?"), so it is good for teaching the rules of selection for antonyms and synonyms, as well as pronouns, prepositions, etc. Lexical paraphrasing (d) involves restating sentences by substituting one or more words, so it is also a good format for teaching synonyms (e.g. "Give me another word for...." after presenting a sentence) and antonyms. Since (b) is not as applicable to the purpose of teaching antonyms and synonyms, answer (e), all of these, is incorrect.

39. D: Divergent thinking (d) is not a tendency or characteristic that would cause difficulty with semantics. Being able to generate a greater variety of alternatives would facilitate ease with semantics. Concrete thinking (a) would contribute to difficulty with semantics as the ability to think abstractly is important to interpreting meanings. Similarly, literal thinking (b) would cause difficulty in interpreting figurative meanings. Limited imagery (c) would interfere, as would limitations in the ability to use symbols and to conceptualize, since these all require some degree of abstraction and imagination. Narrow perception (e) would interfere with semantic ability in that sticking to only one referent for words or concepts, retaining narrow meanings for words, and not shifting from one semantic-grammatical category to another would all prevent someone from identifying multiple and alternative meanings. Another thing that would interfere with semantics is a limited ability to accomplish simultaneously the logical operations, analyses, and syntheses needed for interpreting spatial, temporal, and other relationships among words, phrases, and clauses.

40. B: The Auditory Sequential subtest of the Illinois Test of Psycholinguistic Abilities (b), or ITPA, tests immediate recall of digit series forward *only*. The Numerical Memory scale of the McCarthy Scales (a) and the Digit Span subtest of the Wechsler Intelligence Scales for Children (c) or WISC-IV both test immediate recall of spoken digit series *both* forward and backward. Since (b) is correct, answers (d), none of these, and (e), all of these, are both incorrect.

41. E: In audiology, MCL stands for Most Comfortable Loudness (e). This is the volume at which sound is neither too loud nor too quiet. In audiological examinations, the measure in decibels (dB) assigned to an individual's hearing threshold reflects a loudness at which that person can hear a pure tone *half* of the time. Therefore, we may still be able to hear sounds at a quieter level than we prefer, yet we feel uncomfortable with that level. Conversely, some sounds may not be loud enough to damage our hearing, yet we are still uncomfortable if we find them too loud. Maximum Comfort Level (a) and Minimum Clarity Locutions (b) are invented choices. Medial Collateral Ligaments (c) are real, but are ligaments found in the knee joints. Media Convergence Lab (d) is also real, but it is not associated with the field of audiology. It is a laboratory of the Institute for Simulation and Training at the University of Central Florida in Orlando devoted to creating interactive simulated experiences.

42. B: An audiogram with a sharp "notch" or "bite" showing a drop in acuity around 4,000 Hz, with the other frequencies above and below 4,000 showing a higher, flat line, indicates noise-induced hearing loss (b) in its early stages. Exposure to loud noise destroys nerve fibers that receive the 4,000-Hz frequency. A normal hearing curve (a) would show a relatively flat line across all frequencies, with the dB level close to 0, within a range from -10 dB to 25 dB, the standard for normal hearing. Conductive hearing losses (c) tend to show an audiogram curve that is relatively flat, similar to a normal hearing curve except that the dB level is not within normal range (for example, it could be 50 or 80 dB instead of 0 dB). Age-related hearing losses (d) or presbycusis are the most common form of hearing loss. Their audiograms are often described as "ski-slope loss" for their resemblance to a downhill curve, with hearing being best at the low frequencies and dropping at higher frequencies. The downward curve from left to right may be gradual with smaller decreases in acuity from one frequency to the next (higher) frequency; or it may be very steep in cases of the most extreme loss at the highest frequencies; or it may be anything in between.

43. A: The stapedius (a) is not one of the ossicles, though it is attached to one. "Ossicles" means "little bones." These tiny bones in the middle ear perform the function of conducting sound from the external auditory meatus to the inner ear. They are the stapes (b) or stirrup, the malleus (c) or hammer, and the incus (d) or anvil. When sound enters the ear, the malleus strikes the incus, vibrating the stapes. The stapedius (a) is a muscle that attaches to the stapes. In the event of a sudden, very loud sound, the stapedius muscle pulls the stapes away from the incus, keeping the middle and inner ear from registering the full loudness and protecting against sustaining noise-induced hearing loss. This action by the stapedius muscle is called the stapedius reflex. Since (a) is not one of the ossicles, answer (e), they all are, is incorrect.

44. C: Exposure to excessively loud noises (c) would not cause a conductive hearing loss but a sensorineural hearing loss. Conductive hearing losses are caused when something interferes with the conduction of sound waves to the inner ear where they are converted to electrical energy and sent along the auditory nerve to the brain. Conductive hearing loss is due to any dysfunction of the outer or middle ear while the inner ear is intact. Obstruction by a foreign body (a) such as wax is one cause of conductive hearing loss. Perforation of the tympanic membrane (b) or eardrum would prevent it from vibrating and cause a conductive hearing loss. Rupture would have the same effect as perforation. Damage to one or more of the ossicles (d) that prevented vibration would also stop the conduction process, causing conductive hearing loss. Infections in the middle ear can cause conductive losses due to inflammation and/or fluid or pus. There are also many other causes. Conductive losses can usually be remedied, either improving the hearing or completely restoring it. Sensorineural losses have until recent years been permanent and irreversible, but the cochlear implant now replaces permanently destroyed hair cells for people with profound sensorineural hearing loss and a functioning auditory nerve.

45. B: Damage to one or more ossicles (b) is not a source of sensorineural hearing loss but a source of conductive hearing loss (see #44). Damage to any of the middle ear's tiny bones, stopping them from vibrating and sending sound through the oval and round windows to the inner ear, will impede conduction of sound and cause conductive hearing loss. Destruction of hair cells in the cochlea (a) is a source of sensorineural hearing loss. It can be caused by sudden or ongoing exposure to excessively loud noises (c), by disease or infection, or as a result of aging (d). Since all choices except for (d) are sources of sensorineural hearing loss, answer (e), none of these, is incorrect.

46. D: A Békésy audiometer does not test many more frequencies than usual (a). It does, however, allow subjects to test their own hearing (b) by pressing a button when they hear the tone and holding it down until they no longer hear it. This has diagnostic value in differentiating acoustic neurinoma or other nerve problems from problems in the cochlea, as thresholds determined with continuous tones can be compared to thresholds determined with interrupted tones. The Békésy audiometer can present tones continuously with gradually increasing and decreasing intensity (c). Conventional audiometers present each tone, at each intensity selected by the examiner, one at a time. Researchers found that people with tumors on CN VIII experienced exaggerated adaptation to continuous presentation of fixed frequencies but not to pulsed or interrupted presentations. They found that people with sensorineural losses that were cochlear in origin did not show this extreme adaptation effect. Because (d) is correct, answer (e), all of these, is incorrect.

47. C: UCL in audiology refers to uncomfortable loudness level (c). This is the level of intensity (loudness) at which a sound becomes uncomfortable to an individual. Answers (a) and (b) are invented choices. Upper confidence limit and upper confidence level (d) are terms used in inferential statistical analysis. Confidence levels have to do with margins of error in statistics, not audiology. Universal Communications Language (e) is a term used in information technology (IT) with computers, not in audiology.

48. A: In audiology, recruitment means (a) reduced range between an individual's hearing threshold, most comfortable loudness (MCL) and uncomfortable loudness level (UCL). In individuals with normal hearing, the hearing threshold, MCL and UCL are spread far enough apart to tolerate a wide range of loudness levels without discomfort and still hear the stimulus. People with sensorineural hearing loss are more likely to experience recruitment, so there is a much smaller range within which they hear without uncomfortable loudness. Someone who asks a speaker to speak louder and then becomes irritated because the speaker is 'shouting' actually has a very small difference between sounds too soft to here and those so loud they hurt. Recruitment is frustrating for both speaker and hearer as the hearer needs a narrow range of loudness in order to understand what is said without discomfort. The term recruitment does not refer to the phenomenon that at times, nerves or brain tissue can be substituted to serve the same function as the usual tissues when these are damaged (b). It does not refer to the ability of normal hearing acuity to focus well enough to capture barely audible sounds (c). It does not refer to recruiting the assistance of other people when no hearing aid is available (d). And it does not refer to a wider than normal range between threshold and MCL (e).

49. D: Antoine is likely to have some attentional or neurological deficiencies. The fact that he always starts out responding normally to the sound stimuli indicates that he can hear

them, which eliminates symptoms of organic hearing loss (c). It may be that his attention wanders after a few minutes, or some neurological abnormality may cause him to cease noticing sound stimuli after a few minutes. Though malingering (a) is not impossible it is unlikely due to Antoine's young age and the absence of complaints that he can't hear when spoken to. From interviews and other measures, Antoine also does not demonstrate the knowledge, understanding, sophistication, or initiative to try to manipulate adults or the system this way. He does not display any other attention-seeking behaviors. He is not suffering from hysterical conversion deafness (b) because he does not display any hearing loss with others' speech or other auditory stimuli, and responds normally for the first few minutes of the hearing tests. Deafness by conversion hysteria would result in a uniform failure to respond to auditory stimuli. Because (d) is the most likely answer, answer (e), not likely any of these, is incorrect.

50. E: Presbycusis, or age-related hearing loss, is most often characterized by (e) more hearing loss at higher frequencies. More loss at lower frequencies (a) is not typical of hearing loss associated with aging and is unusual in general. More loss at middle frequencies (b) is also unusual. While early noise-induced hearing loss can cause a sharp drop in acuity around 4,000 Hz (see #42), this is not so much a middle frequency as a medium-high frequency. Uniform loss at all frequencies (c) is not characteristic of presbycusis specifically or of sensorineural losses in general, but is more often found with conductive hearing losses. Having no particular pattern of dB levels at different frequencies (d) is definitely not characteristic of presbycusis. It is also difficult to imagine, since all curves show some kind of pattern, whether it is composed of higher and/or lower levels of acuity at different frequencies or a flat line. With presbycusis, the higher the frequency, the more loss is seen. This accounts for the difficulty people with age-related hearing loss have with discrimination of words containing high-frequency consonant sounds such as /s/, /t/, /f/, etc.

51. A: Dysarthria is a neurologically caused articulation disorder (a). Damage to the parts of the central nervous system controlling the muscles used for speech is the origin of dysarthria. A learning disability affecting reading (b) is dyslexia. A neurologically caused swallowing disorder (c) is dysphagia. An articulation disorder due to dysfunction of the speech organs (d) rather than of the brain is called dyslalia. In general, speech defects related to mental impairment (e) are called dyslogia.

52. B: Open-bite (b) in which the upper and lower teeth do not meet is the *most* likely cause of distorted sibilant consonants /s/, /z/, / ʃ/, and /ʒ/. Overbite (a) or supraclusion usually does not cause consonant distortion. Underbite (c) or mandibular protraction, also called mesioclusion, causes no speech distortions when mild. Even when severe, the tongue and lips can usually adjust to accommodate it. A protruding mandible can sometimes cause sibilant distortion, but it is not as frequent. This type of malocclusion can also cause distortion of /f/ and /v/ consonants. Cross-bite (d) can make it harder to produce sibilants by placing the tongue in a poor position for it, but is not as likely to cause distortion except when it co-exists with other problems such as open-bite, motor problems with the tongue, or malformed dental arches. Collapsed bite (e) can prevent the adult back teeth from erupting completely and force the tongue backward. This can lead to complications with the tonsils and adenoids but is not as likely to cause sibilant distortion.

53. D: The best definition of motor apraxia among the choices given is that (d) he cannot control his external speech organs. For example, when asked to make an /m/ sound, someone with motor apraxia is unable to. When the SLP models using thumb and forefinger to pinch the lips together, Willie will be able to imitate, but he cannot voluntarily press his lips together without the aid of his hand. If he walked as if he were drunk (a), it is a sign of *ataxia* rather than apraxia. If he used his upper but not lower body (b), it is hemiplegia. If his upper and lower body were both paralyzed (c), it is quadriplegia. If he can speak but not understand speech (e), it indicates Wernicke's aphasia or receptive aphasia. None of these other conditions exist in this case. Apraxia means loss of ability to make simple voluntary acts, *especially* loss of ability to perform simple units of action in expressive language.

54. C: This patient is most likely to have oropharyngeal dysphagia (c). Dysphagia is difficulty swallowing. Oropharyngeal is a type of dysphagia most often caused by cerebrovascular strokes or other neurological etiologies such as MS, MG, ALS, Parkinson's disease or Bell's palsy. It can also be caused by radiation, neurotoxins, neck tumors, and other medical conditions. Esophageal dysphagia (a) is not caused by strokes. It can have functional or mechanical etiologies, and is most often caused by cancers in or near the esophagus, or by cancers in the pharynx or stomach. Functional dysphagia (a) describes dysphagia with no known cause. This is not the case here as Mrs. Stokes had a stroke. Esophageal achalasia (d) differs from dysphagias in that there is more difficulty with swallowing liquids than solids. It is characterized by failure of peristalsis along the entire length of the esophagus, by failure of the lower esophageal sphincter to relax sufficiently, and by functional narrowing of the lower esophagus. Though primary achalasia, the most common type, is due to failure of esophageal neurons, the cause of this failure is not known. Odynophagia (e) is pain upon swallowing and is often a symptom of carcinoma.

55. E: Therapy for dysphagia (see # 54) includes all of these (e). Lip exercises (a) increase strength and coordination of the lips, which are important for moving food around the mouth and for creating a tight seal when swallowing. Tongue exercises (b) are helpful because the tongue also moves food around the mouth as the lips do, plus the tongue helps create a bolus of food to be more easily swallowed. Also, the tongue transports the food bolus backward to the pharynx where it can be moved into the esophagus. It is not unusual for a stroke to impair the tongue's mobility. Jaw exercises (c) are also helpful because strokes frequently damage the brain areas that control chewing muscles. This in turn can make it hard to create a bolus of food that is small enough and soft enough to swallow. Swallowing exercises (d) obviously are indicated for swallowing difficulty, especially when this is the result of a stroke. (See #56 for more on swallowing exercises.)

56. B: Like the Shaker exercise, the hyoid lift maneuver (b) does not involve swallowing. In this exercise, a sheet of paper placed on a towel is picked up by sucking on a straw and moved to a container into which it is dropped by the release of suction. The goal is to move several sheets of paper into the container in each session. The Mendelsohn maneuver (a) involves consciously keeping the larynx lifted, while swallowing. This exercise is to be repeated several times a day. The effortful swallow (c) involves swallowing while squeezing the swallowing muscles as hard as possible. Three sets per day are done, with each set consisting of 5-10 attempts. The supraglottic swallow (d) involves holding the breath while swallowing, then coughing (to clear anything that

went down past the vocal cords). It is to be done first without food and can be done with food later as proficiency increases. The super supraglottic swallow maneuver (e) is done like the supraglottic swallow, with the addition of bearing down while swallowing and holding the breath. These exercises strengthen the swallowing muscles.

57. A: In Piaget's theory of cognitive development, sensorineural (a) is not one of the stages. Sensorineural is most often an adjective used to describe a type of hearing loss. Piaget's first stage of cognitive development is the sensorimotor (b) stage. In this stage the infant learns about the environment through sensory input received and motor outputs made to act upon the environment. A milestone during this stage is the achievement of object permanence, the understanding that something exists even when it is not in your presence. Piaget's second stage is the preoperational (c) stage. In this stage the young child cannot yet perform mental operations, but the child's use of symbols and language is accelerated. In Piaget's third stage, concrete operations (d), the child can perform mental operations with concrete objects, such as conservation and class inclusion tasks. The child gains in logical thinking and being able to understand another's point of view, but cannot think abstractly. Abstract thinking is achieved in Piaget's fourth stage of formal operations (e). Preteens and teens can think about hypothetical situations and the future, understand abstract terms such as justice or patriotism, can perform mathematical operations, and can classify things into categories.

58. C: Vygotsky formulated a theory of cognitive development based on sociocultural influences. What he termed "private speech" is when children talk to themselves to direct their own behavior (c). He said that once children have acquired language and learned the rules of their culture, they start using private speech. When they are young, we often hear them talking to themselves aloud as they guide themselves through cognitive activities. Vygotsky said that as children grow older, they continue private speech, but it becomes silent as they internalize it. Even adults talk to themselves aloud, a sign that private speech never goes away but is just internalized. Private speech is not a sign of psychological disturbance (a). It does not refer to private discussions between two close friends (b) or among several intimate friends (d). And it does not mean talking about private subjects rather than public topics (e).

59. E: Surprisingly, researchers (Zimmerman, Christakis, & Meltzoff, 2007) found that children who watch "brain stimulation" videos actually learn words more slowly than babies who do not watch videos, whose parents read to them, or whose parents watch the videos with them and talk about what they are watching (e). Therefore it is not true that babies watching such videos were found to learn new words more rapidly than those not watching them (a) but the opposite. Since word acquisition is slower in the video-watching babies, it is not true that they learn words at the same rate as children whose parents read to them (b). Since video-watching babies learn faster not only when read to by parents but also when parents watch and talk about the videos with them, it is not true that they learn at the same rate whether parents discuss the videos or not (c). Video-watching babies do not learn words faster than children whose parents read to them (d).

60. D: Learning theory focuses only on observable behaviors (d). This is why learning theory is also called behavioral theory. B. F. Skinner, a pioneer of learning theory and behavior modification, maintained that what was going on internally in a subject did not matter, not because internal processes and states did not exist, but because they could

not be observed or measured and therefore could not be changed in a reliable, measurable way. Unconscious impulses (a) were the focus of Freud's psychoanalytic theory and neo-Freudian theories. Freud believed that the majority of the personality was internalized and hidden, even to oneself. Attempts to understand the unconscious were made through "talk" therapy or analysis of patient interviews, including introspection, free association, slips of the tongue, and dream analysis and interpretation. Internal mechanisms (b), such as Freud's ego defense mechanisms, Chomsky's language acquisition device, and other mechanisms described by other theories, are disregarded in learning theory as they are not outwardly demonstrated or observable. Social relationships (c) are the focus of Erikson's psychosocial theory of development, Vygotsky's theory of sociocultural learning, Bandura's social-cognitive theory and others, but not of learning theory. Behavioral theorists like Skinner would assert that social relationships could be changed in practice by the application of behavior modification principles, but the focus of the theory itself is behavior, not social relationships. Since only (d) is correct, answer (e), all these, is incorrect.

61. B: Systematic desensitization uses the technique of (b) successive approximations of exposure to an aversive stimulus. By introducing controlled exposure in small increments or steps, the aversive stimulus is more tolerable to the individual. As the individual becomes less sensitive to a small amount of the stimulus, the next step is taken or increment is added. When the client is allowed to become comfortable with each small step before continuing, this procedure can do much to help overcome, for example, phobias (and may be combined with anti-anxiety medication). It can also be useful in cases of stuttering with strong psychological components. Shaping and chaining are behavioral methods that use successive approximations. Exposure to excessive amounts of the aversive stimulus (a) is a technique called flooding and is the opposite of systematic desensitization. Extinction of an undesirable response (c) is the technique of ignoring the response until the individual no longer engages in it. This typically only works with attention-seeking behaviors. If attention does not reinforce a given behavior, ignoring that behavior will not extinguish it. Since only (b) is correct, answers (d), these are all techniques used, and (e), none of these is, are both incorrect.

62. D: The mother and teacher should be told that (d) Wendy is normal developmentally, because norms for correct consonant articulation vary depending on the specific consonant, and the norm for consistently producing /r/ correctly is around eight years of age. Wendy is only five, so she should not be expected to be able to say /r/ correctly yet. Therefore it cannot be assumed that she has an articulation disorder needing speech therapy (a). Wendy's /w/ for /r/ substitution is not idiolectal because she is not the only child to do this; it is not unusual but quite common (b). It is one of the most common errors by children in this age group, as /r/ is one of the most difficult consonants to produce correctly, which is why it has one of the highest age norms. While it is true that in those with hearing impairment, /r/ is also one of the most common sounds to be produced incorrectly, this does not automatically mean that Wendy has a hearing loss (c). A speech-language pathologist would test her hearing as part of her evaluation, so any hearing loss would be identified, but her developmentally normal articulation error does not mean that she *must* have hearing loss. Because (d) is correct, answer (e), none of these, is incorrect.

63. C: Elise's success is most likely due to a combination of Glenda's therapy and Elise's maturation. From third to fourth grade, Elise's vocal apparatus and central nervous

system have matured, making her speech more amenable to correction. Additionally, last year's SLP did not try using a physical aid to help interrupt Elise's habitual palatalization (which could have been an incorrect learned behavior, a physiological reflex, or both) and reposition her tongue, nor help her become familiar with how the correct position felt until she could reproduce it. Thus it is not likely that Elise's correction is due only to maturation or that the treatment did not help (a). She continued to produce the distorted sound until Glenda tried the tongue depressor; thereafter her articulation improved quickly. While Glenda's idea deserves credit, it cannot be said that it was entirely responsible for the results (b) as maturation probably enhanced Elise's ability to respond to the treatment. To say that success was due to a choice Elise made (d) is unfounded; there is much evidence to the contrary. It is equally unlikely that the correction was sheer luck (e).

64. A: Glenda's age placed her around the developmental norm for correct /r/ production. Once motivated, her self-practice accelerated her progress, and maturationally she was close enough that it was not physiologically impossible for her. It is also correct in (a) that she did not have a "speech impediment," which today would be called an articulation disorder. Moreover, rounded /r/ is a characteristic of some regional dialects. While it is true that Glenda's high IQ facilitated her self-correction without therapy, it is not true that she did have an articulation disorder (b) to overcome. It is not true that Glenda was past the age for correct /r/ production; she started school early, as she was seven in third grade. It is not true that she needed the "push" of being insulted (c). Though Glenda's anger motivated her, she would have responded equally well to more positive correction. Until it was pointed out, she did not hear her own error. It is not true that she deliberately distorted her speech and only changed it to "show" the adults (d). Since (a) is correct, answer (e), none of these, is incorrect.

65. C: The most common form of stuttering is (c) developmental stuttering. When young children are still developing speech and language skills, they may stutter. Some scientists believe that this is due to a child's cognitive and verbal development outpacing that child's speech and language development. Neurogenic stuttering (a) is not as common as developmental stuttering but more common than psychogenic stuttering (b). Neurogenic stuttering is a result of a neurological problem. This can be caused by head trauma, cerebrovascular stroke, or other brain injuries. The stuttering arises from an impaired ability of the brain to coordinate speech actions by properly controlling the muscles and/or nerves involved. Psychogenic stuttering (b) is a result of emotional trauma, emotional problems, mental disorders, and/or cognitive impairments. In the past, stuttering was believed to be always psychogenic in origin. However, now that more research has been done, it has been found that psychogenic stuttering is actually not common. As only (c) is correct, answers (d), both (b) and (c); and (e), all are equally common, are both incorrect.

66. E: Stuttering involves disorders with (e) all of these. Rate (a) refers to the speed at which one speaks. Many stutterers speak too fast. Others slow or stop their speech in their struggle to get the words out. Slowing down can often help stutterers in combination with other strategies. However, when some stutterers struggle too hard to get a word out without repetition or prolongation, the tension can cause blocking, i.e. their speech is completely stopped, which is counterproductive. Many stutterers also show disordered speech rhythms (b), alternately speeding up and slowing down,

prolonging vowel or consonant sounds, or having parts—words, phrases, or sentences—within their overall speech flow that are faster or slower than what sounds normal. Fluency (c) refers to the speaker's ability to speak easily without undue effort and with normal rate and rhythm. There is a class of stutterers known as "fluent stutterers" who do stutter but without interrupting, slowing, or stopping their speech. These are usually mild stutterers. However, stuttering more often does interfere with a speaker's fluency; in fact, stuttering is also referred to as dysfluency or disfluency. Since (e) is correct, answer (d), none of these, is incorrect.

67. D: It is not true that (d) stuttering always lasts for several years in children. Of the approximately 5% of those who will stutter at some time in their lives (e), some will stutter for only a few weeks, others for several years, or it may last for any length of time in between. It is true that about 3 million Americans stutter (a) and that they may be of any age (b). It is true that stuttering occurs most frequently between the ages of 2 and 5 years (c) when children's speech and language abilities are still developing.

68. B: It is not true that fewer boys are likely to stutter as they age (b). In fact, boys are twice as likely to stutter as girls are (a), and the numbers of boys who continue to stutter as they get older is three to four times as many as girls who continue to stutter as they get older. It is true that the majority of children outgrow stuttering (c), and that only around 1% or fewer of adults stutter (d). Since (b) is not true, answer (e), all of these statements are true, is incorrect.

69. A: The only true statement is that (a) three genes causing stuttering have now been isolated. This was done for the first time by researchers at the National Institute on Deafness and other Communication Disorders (NIDCD) in 2010. It is therefore not true that only one gene has been identified (b). It is not true that developmental stuttering is not found to run in families (c); researchers have found that developmental stuttering is more frequent in members of the same family. It is also not true that stuttering that runs in a family is attributed to environmental factors (d) such as reinforcement. Developmental stuttering running in families is attributed to genetic factors, which is supported by the recent isolation of genes causing some cases of it (a). Since (a) is true, answer (e), none of these is true, is incorrect.

70. E: All of these can be used in stuttering therapy (e). Stuttering modification (a) is learning better ways of managing the existing stuttering behaviors. Fluency shaping (b) is learning new speech behaviors that are "fluency-embedded." Both address the overt aspects of stuttering. Changing secondary covert aspects (c) is modifying or adjusting the emotions and attitudes that the stutterer has developed in reaction to the stuttering. Since (e) is correct, answer (d), none of these, is incorrect.

71. C: It is not true in Starkweather's model that (c) stressors in the social environment do not influence speech demands. Social stressors are an important factor, according to Starkweather. Speech is a social behavior. Starkweather states that stressors, or demands, in the social environment can trigger stuttering when those demands exceed the capacity of the individual to speak fluently and continuously (b). These demands trigger the stuttering rather than causing it; Starkweather believes that some people have a predisposition for speech breakdowns (a). These predispositions are thought to be genetic in some people (see also #69), while in others they may not be hereditary but

- 94 -

are results of weaknesses in the speech process involving muscular control, motor coordination, word finding, sentence formation, or auditory monitoring. It is true that most stutterers report that their speech is "just fine" a lot of the time (d), but will stutter in stressful situations such as talking to a superior, talking on the phone, making a presentation, or in a job interview. Since (c) is not true, answer (e), all of these are true, is incorrect.

72. D: Avoidances (d) are not overt or core features of stuttering; they are covert. Avoidances include substituting another word for one with an initial sound that is difficult for the speaker. Pausing before beginning a difficult word is another form of avoidance. Circumlocution, paraphrasing or "talking around" a difficult word or phrase by describing it in other terms is another type of avoidance. Blocks (a) are overt features of stuttering. These occur when the speaker's larynx, vocal folds, lips, and/or tongue become so tense that airflow is stopped or blocked. The speaker appears "stuck." Tremors (b) occur when the jaw is so tense that it begins to quiver rapidly. Tremors are also overt features of stuttering. Repetitions (c) involving a single phoneme, e.g. "P-p-p-p-p-person"; syllable, e.g. "wha-wha-wha-wha-what"; or word, e.g. "It would be impossible to-to-to-to-to" are overt features of stuttering. Prolongations (e) are drawing out the length of a sound, e.g. "Mmmmmother" or "sssssssister," and they are also overt features of stuttering.

73. E: (a) is only true about singing in that the tempo, rhythm, and pitch of a song are all predetermined for the singer, so there are specific limits imposed on the singer's control, and (b) is true for both reciting poems and singing in that both reciting involve preset words as opposed to propositional speech, in which extemporaneous words are required. Severe stutterers may stutter when reading aloud, but it is often easier to read poetry than prose, especially when the poem has a regular rhythm and rhymes. This makes a poem similar to a song except that it does not have preassigned pitches. An absence of stuttering with predetermined words, rate, and rhythm, and also pitch in singing, is not attributed to the enjoyment of reciting poetry or singing a song (c). However, for those who stutter, knowing in advance what words they will use removes much of the stress inherent in having to speak in front of a group. So even if these are not activities they enjoy, they still provide means of controlling one's output such that stuttering does not occur. Since (e) is correct, answer (d), none of these, is incorrect.

74. A: This is an example of a behavioral objective written for speech awareness (a). If met, it will demonstrate that John is aware of his dysfluencies 90% of the time. An example of a behavioral objective written for speech description (b) would be: "When asked by the therapist, John will correctly identify the type and place of dysfluency eight out of ten times." This goes beyond awareness to being able to describe the dysfluencies specifically. An example of a behavioral objective written for speech modification (c) would be: "John will implement Speech Target X in three out of four dysfluencies without cueing." (In reality the X would be replaced by the number or letter identifying one of the listed targets developed for that individual client.) This goes beyond awareness and description to independently using a learned technique to modify, or change, one's speech when dysfluency occurs. An example of a behavioral objective written for speech preparation (d) would be: "John will implement Speech Target X without cueing before initiating words he expects to stutter on three out of four times."

This goes beyond modifying speech when it becomes dysfluent to preventing the dysfluency by implementing a strategy in advance of stuttering.

75. B: This is an example of a behavioral objective written for a stutterer in the area of (b) emotional awareness. If met, it will show that John is aware of his anxiety and the associated symptoms in this type of situation. An example of a behavioral objective for emotional exploration (a) is: "When asked by the therapist, John will describe in detail three childhood experiences that triggered negative emotions." Once he is aware of his emotions related to stuttering, John can explore them to see how they may have developed and been compounded over time. An example of emotional modification (c) is: "On three separate occasions, before speaking to a group, John will pause, take a deep breath, slowly exhale, and attend to the release of muscle tension in one part of his body." This is a part of progressive relaxation practice. Once John recognizes his emotional reactions, he can practice changing them by focusing on the physical tension they cause and releasing it. The effects are reciprocal; just as anxiety causes muscular tension, releasing that tension reduces the anxiety. An example of a behavioral objective written for the area of emotional understanding (d) is: "With the therapist's assistance, John will form one plausible reason for his stuttering and will express it to someone outside of therapy." This reflects gaining insight into reasons for stuttering.

76. C: Non-standard English. In Black English, Southern White non-standard English, and other non-standard English dialects, these are all common utterances. "He bad" demonstrates the absence of the copula "is" whenever it can be a contraction in Standard English and is common in Black and White non-standard English. "Where was you?" demonstrates lack of subject-verb agreement with respect to person number and is used by Black and White non-standard English speakers. "That Renee toy" demonstrates omission of the possessive ['s] when word order indicates possession. This is common in Black English and tends to be consistent in Southern speakers, while northern urban speakers may alternate between using the ['s] ending or relying on word order. "She don't drive" uses what is the plural form of the auxiliary verb "do" in Standard English instead of the singular "does" when the construction is negative ("don't" instead of "doesn't"). This is common in both Black and White non-standard English. "I knowed that" is using the regular "-ed" past tense ending with irregular verbs instead of, for example, the correct vowel change ("know-knew," "freeze-froze," "drink-drank," etc.) and is a feature of non-standard English. These expressions are not due to delayed language development (a). Delayed language development typically results in incorrect word order; incorrect prepositions; incorrect pronouns; limited vocabulary; and misuse of synonyms and antonyms. They are not attributable to disorders of articulation (b) as they are differences in morphology, not in speech sound production or pronunciation. Since (c) is correct, answers (d), none of these, and (e), all of these, are incorrect.

77. E: All of these are parts (e) of a lesson plan for speech-language therapy in a school setting. Goals for the semester (a) are more general or global. A student will usually have about three goals to work on over the semester. These may be revised during the semester as needed, for example, if the student makes such great progress that they no longer apply, or if new information is discovered. Behavioral objectives (b) are ways to achieve the goals. They specifically describe what behaviors the student is expected to perform during a given activity. They can often be changed or adjusted as often as weekly according to the student's performance. The activities the student is to engage in should be described (c) briefly in a lesson plan to give an idea of what you are planning, but not in great detail. You should also list the materials to be used (d) during each separate activity in your lesson plan.

78. B: Researchers did not find that (b) differences in the articulation of those with surgically repaired clefts and those with unrepaired clefts were very large. While those with unrepaired cleft palates did have worse articulation than those with surgical repair, the differences were not large. One study found a difference of only .17 between the mean ratios of obtained scores to norms for subjects with and without surgical repair of cleft palates. Another study found a difference of 25%, i.e. 54% correct articulation for subjects with unrepaired clefts and 79% correct articulation for subjects with repaired clefts. Researchers did find that those with cleft lip only but not cleft palate have basically normal articulation (a). They found that unilateral clefts, i.e. clefts on only one side, allowed better articulation of speech sounds than bilateral or two-sided clefts (c). They also found that those with incomplete clefts had better articulation than those with complete clefts (d). Since (b) was not a finding, answer (e), all of these, is incorrect.

79. A: Research has found that people with cleft palates consistently have the highest rates of correct production of (a) nasal consonants like /m/, /n/, and /ŋ/. This makes sense when one considers that one of the byproducts of cleft palate is hypernasality. It would follow that it is easier for people whose speech is already nasal to produce nasal consonants correctly. The second highest ranking of correct articulation for those with cleft palate was (b) glides or semivowels like /r/, /l/, /j/, or /w/; the third was (c) plosives or stops like /p/, /b/, /t/, /k/; ranked fourth highest were (e) fricatives like /θ/, /ð/, /s/, /z/, /f/, /v/; and fifth were (d) affricates like /tʃ/ or /dʒ/.

80. D: Daniel R. Boone (d) of the University of Arizona specializes in voice disorders and voice therapy, not stuttering. George H. Shames (a), professor emeritus of the University of Pittsburgh, was director of the university's speech clinic for 40 years and a licensed clinical psychologist, and specialized in stuttering. He developed "Stutter-Free Speech" and invented three biofeedback devices for stuttering. Shames was influenced by Charles G. Van Riper (b), a lifelong severe stutterer himself, who founded the speech clinic at Western Michigan State Normal School in Kalamazoo, and was the first chair of the school's speech pathology and audiology department. Martin F. Schwartz (c) from NYU Medical Center was a researcher in cleft lip and cleft palate surgery who stumbled on neck constriction in stutterers in 1974. Schwartz had been using ultrasound imaging on stutterers and found they had laryngeal spasms, ultimately discovering that the physical origin of stuttering was a reflexive locking of the vocal cords. He then created the passive-inhalation airflow technique of stuttering therapy. He directs the National Center for Stuttering. Gary J. Rentschler (e) is director of the Stuttering Clinic at Duquesne University. He focuses on the roles that emotional and psychosocial issues play in maintaining stuttering.

81. D: Acute infectious laryngitis (d) is not responsive to voice therapy. The infection must be treated then the patient must rest the voice until phonation feels and sounds normal again. Thickening of the vocal cords (a) can result from long-term abuse or misuse of the voice or from chronic infections of the vocal folds. Voice therapy focuses on reducing voice abuse and misuse and reducing or eliminating sources of irritation, such as allergies, smoking, etc. Vocal nodules and vocal polyps (b) are both treated first by surgery, then by complete voice rest, and finally by voice therapy. The same is true of laryngeal contact ulcers (c). Because (d) is correct, answer (e), these all respond, is incorrect.

82. E: All of these (e) cause voice disorders. Laryngeal papilloma (a) is probably the most common of the benign tumors that occur to the larynx during childhood. It is relatively rare after puberty. Laryngeal carcinoma (b) is a malignant cancer that can occur on the larynx. Unless detected early enough it often requires laryngectomy, or removal of the larynx, to treat it. During puberty the larynx grows (c), and this causes hoarseness and pitch breaks, especially in boys. As these are temporary they do not usually require voice therapy. However, many boys have to abstain from singing until their vocal apparatus stabilizes. Imbalances of the endocrine system can also affect the voice (d) by making the pitch much higher or lower than is normal for the individual's sex and age.

83. C: The least common feature of a functional dysphonia would be (c) an overly loud voice. It is more common in disorders of loudness to find an overly weak, soft, or quiet voice (d). This is thought by some clinicians to reflect shyness, insecurity, and poor interpersonal interactions. Nonetheless, voice therapy to improve respiration and loudness is found more effective than trying to improve the patient's self-esteem and social relationships. Common features of functional dysphonia not related to loudness include breathiness (a), caused by lax approximation of the vocal folds, which may be consistent or only occur with fatigue from overuse; hoarseness (b), also caused by vocal fatigue, from vocal misuse or overuse; and harshness (e), caused by hard vocal attack, over-approximation of the vocal folds, or by a resonance disorder featuring tongue retraction, pharyngeal constriction, and sometimes nasality.

84. B: The disorder most likely to result in no voice at all is (b) functional aphonia because underadducted vocal folds do not touch and will permit only whispering. The most common form of spastic dysphonia (a) involves overadduction of the vocal folds, bringing them together tightly so air cannot easily escape, resulting in a strained, choked or creaky voice. A less common form of spastic dysphonia features abduction and causes sudden moments of breathiness or momentary loss of voice in the midst of phonation when the glottis widens. Vocal cord paralysis (c) can cause hoarseness, breathiness, loss of intensity, and loss of pitch range. In ventricular dysphonia (d) the patient adducts and vibrates the ventricular bands instead of or in addition to the vocal cords. In patients with intact vocal cords, voice therapy it is effective. However, if the vocal cords are inoperative a ventricular voice is better than no voice. Laryngeal web or synechia (e) can grow between the vocal folds, usually triggered by mucosal surface irritation or laryngeal trauma (injury). It can cause severe dysphonia and shortness of breath, but not a total absence of voice. Treatment is surgery followed by voice therapy to normalize phonation as much as possible.

85. A: A variable not typically rated in a voice screening for school children is (a) rate, or speed of the child's speech. This would be a variable more likely to be evaluated in screening or testing for stuttering, expressive aphasia, or possibly delayed language development. The variables typically rated in voice screenings include (b) pitch, or frequency—how high or low the voice is relative to norms for the child's sex and age; (c) Quality of phonation, or whether the voice is hoarse, breathy, etc.; (d) loudness, or whether the voice sounds softer or louder than normal; and (e) resonance, or whether the voice sounds too nasal (hypernasality), not nasal enough (denasality), or has assimilative nasality, i.e. vowel sounds become more nasal when next to nasal consonants.

86. E: All of these can cause hypernasality (e). A short palate (a) can lead to inadequate velopharyngeal closure, which results in a hypernasal voice. Surgical trauma (b) can also cause velopharyngeal insufficiency and hence hypernasality, as can accidental injury to the soft palate (c). Some diseases can impair the innervation of the soft palate, and such neurological impairment (d) will also result in velopharyngeal insufficiency and hypernasality.

87. C: Patients with structurally inadequate velopharyngeal closure or palatal insufficiency (c) will not benefit from voice therapy. They cannot be taught to improve resonance via training if their equipment does not function to produce enough closure. Those with structural (physical) inadequacies must have surgery or dental treatment (a) to correct them. Once they have had this done, they can benefit from voice therapy, especially if the physical treatment has given them only marginal closure, in which case voice therapy can help them to maximize their use of their phonatory mechanisms. Patients whose hypernasal speech is not structural but functional in etiology (b) can benefit from voice therapy. Their physical mechanism is not inadequate, but they use hypernasal speech for functional reasons (to sound authoritative, to sound like a famous person, or they may have done it at one time and then developed a habit). Because (c) is correct, answers (d), all of these, and (e), none of these, are incorrect.

88. D: Establishing new pitch (d) is used for hypernasality but not denasality. Some people with hypernasal voices speak with overly high pitches, which increases nasality. Speaking at a lower pitch can contribute to greater oral resonance instead of greater nasal resonance. People with denasalized voices sound congested all of the time. The other four therapy approaches listed can be used with both hypernasality and denasality. Feedback (a) helps the patient to become aware of voice sound and how it feels physically to produce it. Thus it applies to both excessive and insufficient nasal resonance. Ear training (b) focuses on increasing the patient's ability to hear the differences between oral resonances and nasal resonances, so it can be used for either decreasing or increasing nasality. The target voice models approach (c) consists of recording the patient's voice whenever it has a good balance of oral and nasal resonance, and playing this back for the patient to hear. The patient's own phonation, when its resonance is closest to ideal, becomes the patient's own model and can be used equally for hypernasality and denasality. The explanation of problem approach (e) involves explaining to the patient before beginning any therapy exactly what the problem is, i.e. that the patient's speech is either overly nasal or not nasal enough (the latter especially with nasal consonants) and is used with either type of problem.

89. A: It is not true that nasal emission is a nasal resonance problem (a). Nasal emission is nasal noise caused by air escaping through the nose when there is incomplete velopharyngeal closure. Though it is not a disorder of nasal resonance per se, it often accompanies hypernasality (b) when the etiology is structural. In addition to weakened movement of the velum and pharynx, a short palate can cause nasal emissions, so these can be symptomatic of palatal insufficiency (c). It is true that nasal emission rarely occurs for functional reasons (d). It is nearly always related to some structural inadequacy. It is also true that nasal emission cannot be remediated by speech therapy alone (e). Usually surgical or prosthodontic intervention is required in addition to and prior to speech therapy.

90. B: Overly high pitches at all ages (b) is not a characteristic of voice differences in deaf speakers. Deaf children around the ages of seven or eight years have not been observed to speak with higher pitches than hearing children. However, as children grow older, those with hearing develop lower-pitched voices after puberty while deaf children do not (a). Researchers have concluded this is because they do not have the auditory feedback that hearing children do and thus cannot acoustically monitor their voices. It has been found that deaf individuals without voice training tend to focus their resonance in their pharynx (c), caused by poor tongue positioning, especially retraction toward the pharyngeal wall, leading to "cul de sac resonance." Severe denasality (d) often results from pharyngeal resonance focus, but there are also some deaf people who display true hypernasality (e) in their voices.

91. E: All of these (e) are prostheses for voice production by laryngectomees. The Blom-Singer (a) is an indwelling low-pressure voice prosthesis kit. The VoiceMaster (b) is a front-loading, indwelling prosthetic device. The ProVox (c) is a low-resistance indwelling prosthetic device made of medical-grade silicone that can be either front-loaded (i.e., inserted through the tracheostoma) or back-loaded through the mouth. Since (e) is correct, answer (d), none of these, is incorrect.

92. C: The Blom-Singer (c) is not an electromechanical voice device but a prosthetic device. Electromechanical devices are not prostheses for the removed speech structures but instead create electromechanical vibrations heard as tones. The patient then manipulates the remaining speech structures (tongue, lips and teeth) the same way as before surgery to alter the tone into different speech sounds. Electromechanical devices are either transcervical or intraoral. The Servox (a) is an electrolarynx which is transcervical, i.e. it is held by hand against the neck. The Cooper-Rand (b) is an intraoral device that generates sound the same way as a transcervical electrolarynx, but introduces the sound source directly into the oral cavity via a tube. Since (c) is the correct answer, answers (d), all of these, and (e), none of these, are incorrect.

93. A: The quality of the voice tone produced (a) is not an advantage of electrolarynx devices. Being electromechanical, they produce a robotic-sounding voice which is perceived as unnatural and distracting to listeners. It is an advantage of these devices that laryngectomy patients can quickly and easily learn to use them (b). This contrasts with the time and effort it takes to learn esophageal speech, for example. Therefore they are a good choice for being able to communicate more immediately while learning other methods, as they do not interfere with or delay this (d). Another advantage of electrolarynx devices is that they produce a loud voice (c) which can be easily heard,

which other methods like esophageal speech may not. Although they are quite expensive, they are still one of the less costly choices (e) compared to others.

94. D: Loudness of the voice tone (d) is not a disadvantage of electrolarynx devices but is an advantage (see #93). Other methods such as esophageal speech may not produce a voice s sufficiently loud to be audible to others. On the other hand, the sound of the voice tone (e) they produce is a disadvantage because of the mechanical, monotonous, robot-like quality that can distract both listeners and speakers. Patients who have had extreme surgery and/or radiation frequently develop fibrosis (scar tissue) of the neck which interferes with the transmission of the tone into the oral cavity, so this is one disadvantage of these devices (a). Also, the patient must use one hand to hold the device, so some manual dexterity is required (b). This is a disadvantage for patients with limited or no manual dexterity; for those with good dexterity, holding the device occupies one hand so it cannot be used for anything else. Another disadvantage of these devices is their conspicuous appearance (c) which can be stigmatizing as well as distracting.

95. B: The HME device is (b) used to protect the airway for respiration. HME stands for Heat and Moisture Exchanger. It is a filter installed to the tracheostoma which captures heat and moisture from the air exhaled through it. Then when the patient inhales, some of this captured heat and moisture are picked up so the patient is not breathing cool, dry outside air. This protects the airway. Total laryngectomy patients have lost the air moisturizing and warming functions of their noses because they now breathe through their necks via a tracheostoma instead of through the nose. This causes mucus to become more viscous, reducing escalator transport. It can also result in excessive phlegm production. The simple HME device restores some of the air conditioning and filtration. The HME is not used to produce a voice, either prosthetically (a) or electromechanically (c). It is only used to condition and filter the air inhaled by the patient. Since (b) is correct, answers (d), none of these, and (e), all of these, are both incorrect.

96. E: All of these are advantages with TEP (e). Compared to other vocal rehabilitation methods such as esophageal speech or the electrolarynx, the silicone prosthesis inserted via the tracheoesophageal puncture technique can produce a better quality of voice tone (a). Patients receiving this treatment have high success rates of achieving a usable voice (b). They are able to achieve this without very much teaching or training (c) by a therapist compared to some other methods like esophageal speech. Because (e) is correct, answer (d), none of these, is incorrect.

97. D: Low resistance to the flow of air (d) is not a disadvantage of TEP-inserted prostheses, but an advantage in that it makes vocal production easier than working against higher airflow resistance. Major disadvantages of this treatment include required daily maintenance (a); recurrent leakage after a period of prosthetic use (b); the need to replace the prosthesis periodically (c); and the expenses associated with this method (e). Another disadvantage is that most patients have to use one hand to block the tracheostoma, similarly to the need to use one hand with an electrolarynx (see #94). Other less frequent complications that can occur with TEP prostheses are the formation of granulomatous tissue at the site, which has been reported in about 5% of cases; and aspiration of the prosthesis itself, which is more serious but occurs in only about 1% to 5% of cases.

98. C: Enlargement of the fistula (c) is not a desirable characteristic of a good voice prosthesis. When a tracheoesophageal fistula (TEF) is surgically created for the insertion of the prosthesis, it should fit snugly around the inserted device. If the fistula becomes larger with time, this leads to leakage around the prosthesis (see #97). According to voice rehabilitation specialists, the characteristics that today's best voice prostheses should have are: (a) safe and reliable use; (b) frontloading insertion, meaning insertion through the tracheostoma rather than the mouth; (d) low resistance to airflow; and (e) semi-permanent fixation, also known as indwelling fixation, whereby the prosthesis has an additional flange to keep it fixed in place so it is not aspirated and does not migrate or move around. This was developed by Panje as a variation of previous prostheses and was refined by Groningen.

Secret Key #1 - Time is Your Greatest Enemy

Pace Yourself

Wear a watch. At the beginning of the test, check the time (or start a chronometer on your watch to count the minutes), and check the time after every few questions to make sure you are "on schedule."

If you are forced to speed up, do it efficiently. Usually one or more answer choices can be eliminated without too much difficulty. Above all, don't panic. Don't speed up and just begin guessing at random choices. By pacing yourself, and continually monitoring your progress against your watch, you will always know exactly how far ahead or behind you are with your available time. If you find that you are one minute behind on the test, don't skip one question without spending any time on it, just to catch back up. Take 15 fewer seconds on the next four questions, and after four questions you'll have caught back up. Once you catch back up, you can continue working each problem at your normal pace.

Furthermore, don't dwell on the problems that you were rushed on. If a problem was taking up too much time and you made a hurried guess, it must be difficult. The difficult questions are the ones you are most likely to miss anyway, so it isn't a big loss. It is better to end with more time than you need than to run out of time.

Lastly, sometimes it is beneficial to slow down if you are constantly getting ahead of time. You are always more likely to catch a careless mistake by working more slowly than quickly, and among very high-scoring test takers (those who are likely to have lots of time left over), careless errors affect the score more than mastery of material.

Secret Key #2 - Guessing is not Guesswork

You probably know that guessing is a good idea - unlike other standardized tests, there is no penalty for getting a wrong answer. Even if you have no idea about a question, you still have a 20-25% chance of getting it right.

Most test takers do not understand the impact that proper guessing can have on their score. Unless you score extremely high, guessing will significantly contribute to your final score.

Monkeys Take the Test

What most test takers don't realize is that to insure that 20-25% chance, you have to guess randomly. If you put 20 monkeys in a room to take this test, assuming they answered once per question and behaved themselves, on average they would get 20-25% of the questions correct. Put 20 test takers in the room, and the average will be much lower among guessed questions. Why?
  1. The test writers intentionally write deceptive answer choices that "look" right. A test taker has no idea about a question, so picks the "best looking" answer, which is often

wrong. The monkey has no idea what looks good and what doesn't, so will consistently be lucky about 20-25% of the time.

2. Test takers will eliminate answer choices from the guessing pool based on a hunch or intuition. Simple but correct answers often get excluded, leaving a 0% chance of being correct. The monkey has no clue, and often gets lucky with the best choice.

This is why the process of elimination endorsed by most test courses is flawed and detrimental to your performance- test takers don't guess, they make an ignorant stab in the dark that is usually worse than random.

$5 Challenge

Let me introduce one of the most valuable ideas of this course- the $5 challenge:

You only mark your "best guess" if you are willing to bet $5 on it.
You only eliminate choices from guessing if you are willing to bet $5 on it.

Why $5? Five dollars is an amount of money that is small yet not insignificant, and can really add up fast (20 questions could cost you $100). Likewise, each answer choice on one question of the test will have a small impact on your overall score, but it can really add up to a lot of points in the end.

The process of elimination IS valuable. The following shows your chance of guessing it right:

If you eliminate wrong answer choices until only this many remain:	Chance of getting it correct:
1	100%
2	50%
3	33%

However, if you accidentally eliminate the right answer or go on a hunch for an incorrect answer, your chances drop dramatically: to 0%. By guessing among all the answer choices, you are GUARANTEED to have a shot at the right answer.

That's why the $5 test is so valuable- if you give up the advantage and safety of a pure guess, it had better be worth the risk.

What we still haven't covered is how to be sure that whatever guess you make is truly random. Here's the easiest way:

Always pick the first answer choice among those remaining.

Such a technique means that you have decided, **before you see a single test question**, exactly how you are going to guess- and since the order of choices tells you nothing about which one is correct, this guessing technique is perfectly random.

This section is not meant to scare you away from making educated guesses or eliminating choices- you just need to define when a choice is worth eliminating. The $5 test, along with a pre-defined random guessing strategy, is the best way to make sure you reap all of the benefits of guessing.

Secret Key #3 - Practice Smarter, Not Harder

Many test takers delay the test preparation process because they dread the awful amounts of practice time they think necessary to succeed on the test. We have refined an effective method that will take you only a fraction of the time.

There are a number of "obstacles" in your way to succeed. Among these are answering questions, finishing in time, and mastering test-taking strategies. All must be executed on the day of the test at peak performance, or your score will suffer. The test is a mental marathon that has a large impact on your future.

Just like a marathon runner, it is important to work your way up to the full challenge. So first you just worry about questions, and then time, and finally strategy:

Success Strategy

1. Find a good source for practice tests.
2. If you are willing to make a larger time investment, consider using more than one study guide- often the different approaches of multiple authors will help you "get" difficult concepts.
3. Take a practice test with no time constraints, with all study helps "open book." Take your time with questions and focus on applying strategies.
4. Take a practice test with time constraints, with all guides "open book."
5. Take a final practice test with no open material and time limits

If you have time to take more practice tests, just repeat step 5. By gradually exposing yourself to the full rigors of the test environment, you will condition your mind to the stress of test day and maximize your success.

Secret Key #4 - Prepare, Don't Procrastinate

Let me state an obvious fact: if you take the test three times, you will get three different scores. This is due to the way you feel on test day, the level of preparedness you have, and, despite the test writers' claims to the contrary, some tests WILL be easier for you than others.
Since your future depends so much on your score, you should maximize your chances of success. In order to maximize the likelihood of success, you've got to prepare in advance. This means taking practice tests and spending time learning the information and test taking strategies you will need to succeed.

Never take the test as a "practice" test, expecting that you can just take it again if you need to. Feel free to take sample tests on your own, but when you go to take the official test, be prepared, be focused, and do your best the first time!

Secret Key #5 - Test Yourself

Everyone knows that time is money. There is no need to spend too much of your time or too little of your time preparing for the test. You should only spend as much of your precious time preparing as is necessary for you to get the score you need.

Once you have taken a practice test under real conditions of time constraints, then you will know if you are ready for the test or not.

If you have scored extremely high the first time that you take the practice test, then there is not much point in spending countless hours studying. You are already there.

Benchmark your abilities by retaking practice tests and seeing how much you have improved. Once you score high enough to guarantee success, then you are ready. If you have scored well below where you need, then knuckle down and begin studying in earnest. Check your improvement regularly through the use of practice tests under real conditions. Above all, don't worry, panic, or give up. The key is perseverance!

Then, when you go to take the test, remain confident and remember how well you did on the practice tests. If you can score high enough on a practice test, then you can do the same on the real thing.

General Strategies

The most important thing you can do is to ignore your fears and jump into the test immediately- do not be overwhelmed by any strange-sounding terms. You have to jump into the test like jumping into a pool- all at once is the easiest way.

Make Predictions

As you read and understand the question, try to guess what the answer will be. Remember that several of the answer choices are wrong, and once you begin reading them, your mind will immediately become cluttered with answer choices designed to throw you off. Your mind is typically the most focused immediately after you have read the question and digested its contents. If you can, try to predict what the correct answer will be. You may be surprised at what you can predict.

Quickly scan the choices and see if your prediction is in the listed answer choices. If it is, then you can be quite confident that you have the right answer. It still won't hurt to check the other answer choices, but most of the time, you've got it!

Answer the Question

It may seem obvious to only pick answer choices that answer the question, but the test writers can create some excellent answer choices that are wrong. Don't pick an answer just because it sounds right, or you believe it to be true. It MUST answer the question. Once you've made your selection, always go back and check it against the question and make sure that you didn't misread the question, and the answer choice does answer the question posed.

Benchmark

After you read the first answer choice, decide if you think it sounds correct or not. If it doesn't, move on to the next answer choice. If it does, mentally mark that answer choice. This doesn't mean that you've definitely selected it as your answer choice, it just means that it's the best you've seen thus far. Go ahead and read the next choice. If the next choice is worse than the one you've already selected, keep going to the next answer choice. If the next choice is better than the choice you've already selected, mentally mark the new answer choice as your best guess.

The first answer choice that you select becomes your standard. Every other answer choice must be benchmarked against that standard. That choice is correct until proven otherwise by another answer choice beating it out. Once you've decided that no other answer choice seems as good, do one final check to ensure that your answer choice answers the question posed.

Valid Information

Don't discount any of the information provided in the question. Every piece of information may be necessary to determine the correct answer. None of the information in the question is there to throw you off (while the answer choices will certainly have information to throw you off). If two seemingly unrelated topics are discussed, don't ignore either. You can be confident there is a relationship, or it wouldn't be included in the question, and you are probably going to have to determine what that relationship is to find the answer.

Avoid "Fact Traps"

Don't get distracted by a choice that is factually true. Your search is for the answer that answers the question. Stay focused and don't fall for an answer that is true but incorrect. Always go back to the question and make sure you're choosing an answer that actually answers the question and is not just a true statement. An answer can be factually correct, but it MUST answer the question asked. Additionally, two answers can both be seemingly correct, so be sure to read all of the answer choices, and make sure that you get the one that BEST answers the question.

Milk the Question

Some of the questions may throw you completely off. They might deal with a subject you have not been exposed to, or one that you haven't reviewed in years. While your lack of knowledge about the subject will be a hindrance, the question itself can give you many clues that will help you find the correct answer. Read the question carefully and look for clues. Watch particularly for adjectives and nouns describing difficult terms or words that you don't recognize. Regardless of if you completely understand a word or not, replacing it with a synonym either provided or one you more familiar with may help you to understand what the questions are asking. Rather than wracking your mind about specific detailed information concerning a difficult term or word, try to use mental substitutes that are easier to understand.

The Trap of Familiarity

Don't just choose a word because you recognize it. On difficult questions, you may not recognize a number of words in the answer choices. The test writers don't put "make-believe" words on the test; so don't think that just because you only recognize all the words in one answer choice means that answer choice must be correct. If you only recognize words in one answer choice, then focus on that one. Is it correct? Try your best to determine if it is correct. If it is, that is great, but if it doesn't, eliminate it. Each word and answer choice you eliminate increases your chances of getting the question correct, even if you then have to guess among the unfamiliar choices.

Eliminate Answers

Eliminate choices as soon as you realize they are wrong. But be careful! Make sure you consider all of the possible answer choices. Just because one appears right, doesn't mean that the next one won't be even better! The test writers will usually put more than one good answer choice for every question, so read all of them. Don't worry if you are stuck between two that seem right. By getting down to just two remaining possible choices, your odds are now 50/50. Rather than wasting too much time, play the odds. You are guessing, but guessing wisely, because you've been able to knock out some of the answer choices that you know are wrong. If you are eliminating choices and realize that the last answer choice you are left with is also obviously wrong, don't panic. Start over and consider each choice again. There may easily be something that you missed the first time and will realize on the second pass.

Tough Questions

If you are stumped on a problem or it appears too hard or too difficult, don't waste time. Move on! Remember though, if you can quickly check for obviously incorrect answer choices, your chances of guessing correctly are greatly improved. Before you completely give up, at least try to knock out a couple of possible answers. Eliminate what you can and then guess at the remaining answer choices before moving on.

Brainstorm

If you get stuck on a difficult question, spend a few seconds quickly brainstorming. Run through the complete list of possible answer choices. Look at each choice and ask yourself, "Could this answer the question satisfactorily?" Go through each answer choice and consider it independently of the other. By systematically going through all possibilities, you may find something that you would otherwise overlook. Remember that when you get stuck, it's important to try to keep moving.

Read Carefully

Understand the problem. Read the question and answer choices carefully. Don't miss the question because you misread the terms. You have plenty of time to read each question thoroughly and make sure you understand what is being asked. Yet a happy medium must be attained, so don't waste too much time. You must read carefully, but efficiently.

Face Value

When in doubt, use common sense. Always accept the situation in the problem at face value. Don't read too much into it. These problems will not require you to make huge leaps of logic. The test writers aren't trying to throw you off with a cheap trick. If you have to go beyond creativity and make a leap of logic in order to have an answer choice answer the question, then you should look at the other answer choices. Don't overcomplicate the problem by creating theoretical relationships or explanations that will warp time or space. These are normal problems rooted in reality. It's just that the applicable relationship or explanation may not be readily apparent and you have to figure things out. Use your common sense to interpret anything that isn't clear.

Prefixes

If you're having trouble with a word in the question or answer choices, try dissecting it. Take advantage of every clue that the word might include. Prefixes and suffixes can be a huge help. Usually they allow you to determine a basic meaning. Pre- means before, post- means after, pro - is positive, de- is negative. From these prefixes and suffixes, you can get an idea of the general meaning of the word and try to put it into context. Beware though of any traps. Just because con is the opposite of pro, doesn't necessarily mean congress is the opposite of progress!

Hedge Phrases

Watch out for critical "hedge" phrases, such as likely, may, can, will often, sometimes, often, almost, mostly, usually, generally, rarely, sometimes. Question writers insert these hedge phrases to cover every possibility. Often an answer choice will be wrong simply because it leaves no room for exception. Avoid answer choices that have definitive words like "exactly," and "always".

Switchback Words

Stay alert for "switchbacks". These are the words and phrases frequently used to alert you to shifts in thought. The most common switchback word is "but". Others include although, however, nevertheless, on the other hand, even though, while, in spite of, despite, regardless of.

New Information

Correct answer choices will rarely have completely new information included. Answer choices typically are straightforward reflections of the material asked about and will directly relate to the question. If a new piece of information is included in an answer choice that doesn't even seem to relate to the topic being asked about, then that answer choice is likely incorrect. All of the information needed to answer the question is usually provided for you, and so you should not have to make guesses that are unsupported or choose answer choices that require unknown information that cannot be reasoned on its own.

Time Management

On technical questions, don't get lost on the technical terms. Don't spend too much time on any one question. If you don't know what a term means, then since you don't have a dictionary, odds are you aren't going to get much further. You should immediately recognize terms as whether or not you know them. If you don't, work with the other clues that you have, the other answer choices and terms provided, but don't waste too much time trying to figure out a difficult term.

Contextual Clues

Look for contextual clues. An answer can be right but not correct. The contextual clues will help you find the answer that is most right and is correct. Understand the context in which a phrase or statement is made. This will help you make important distinctions.

Don't Panic

Panicking will not answer any questions for you. Therefore, it isn't helpful. When you first see the question, if your mind goes blank, take a deep breath. Force yourself to mechanically go through the steps of solving the problem and using the strategies you've learned.

Pace Yourself

Don't get clock fever. It's easy to be overwhelmed when you're looking at a page full of questions, your mind is full of random thoughts and feeling confused, and the clock is ticking down faster than you would like. Calm down and maintain the pace that you have set for yourself. As long as you are on track by monitoring your pace, you are guaranteed to have enough time for yourself. When you get to the last few minutes of the test, it may seem like you won't have enough time left, but if you only have as many questions as you should have left at that point, then you're right on track!

Answer Selection

The best way to pick an answer choice is to eliminate all of those that are wrong, until only one is left and confirm that is the correct answer. Sometimes though, an answer choice may immediately look right. Be careful! Take a second to make sure that the other choices are not equally obvious. Don't make a hasty mistake. There are only two times that you should stop before checking other answers. First is when you are positive that the answer choice you have selected is correct. Second is when time is almost out and you have to make a quick guess!

Check Your Work

Since you will probably not know every term listed and the answer to every question, it is important that you get credit for the ones that you do know. Don't miss any questions through careless mistakes. If at all possible, try to take a second to look back over your answer selection and make sure you've selected the correct answer choice and haven't made a costly careless mistake (such as marking an answer choice that you didn't mean to mark). This quick double check should more than pay for itself in caught mistakes for the time it costs.

Beware of Directly Quoted Answers

Sometimes an answer choice will repeat word for word a portion of the question or reference section. However, beware of such exact duplication – it may be a trap! More than likely, the correct choice will paraphrase or summarize a point, rather than being exactly the same wording.

Slang

Scientific sounding answers are better than slang ones. An answer choice that begins "To compare the outcomes…" is much more likely to be correct than one that begins "Because some people insisted…"

Extreme Statements

Avoid wild answers that throw out highly controversial ideas that are proclaimed as established fact. An answer choice that states the "process should be used in certain situations, if..." is much more likely to be correct than one that states the "process should be discontinued completely." The first is a calm rational statement and doesn't even make a definitive, uncompromising stance, using a hedge word "if" to provide wiggle room, whereas the second choice is a radical idea and far more extreme.

Answer Choice Families

When you have two or more answer choices that are direct opposites or parallels, one of them is usually the correct answer. For instance, if one answer choice states "x increases" and another answer choice states "x decreases" or "y increases," then those two or three answer choices are very similar in construction and fall into the same family of answer choices. A family of answer choices is when two or three answer choices are very similar in construction, and yet often have a directly opposite meaning. Usually the correct answer choice will be in that family of answer choices. The "odd man out" or answer choice that doesn't seem to fit the parallel construction of the other answer choices is more likely to be incorrect.

Special Report: What Your Test Score Will Tell You About Your IQ

Did you know that most standardized tests correlate very strongly with IQ? In fact, your general intelligence is a better predictor of your success than any other factor, and most tests intentionally measure this trait to some degree to ensure that those selected by the test are truly qualified for the test's purposes.

Before we can delve into the relation between your test score and IQ, I will first have to explain what exactly is IQ. Here's the formula:

Your IQ = 100 + (Number of standard deviations below or above the average)*15

Now, let's define standard deviations by using an example. If we have 5 people with 5 different heights, then first we calculate the average. Let's say the average was 65 inches. The standard deviation is the "average distance" away from the average of each of the members. It is a direct measure of variability - if the 5 people included Jackie Chan and Shaquille O'Neal, obviously there's a lot more variability in that group than a group of 5 sisters who are all within 6 inches in height of each other. The standard deviation uses a number to characterize the average range of difference within a group.

A convenient feature of most groups is that they have a "normal" distribution- makes sense that most things would be normal, right? Without getting into a bunch of statistical mumbo-jumbo, you just need to know that if you know the average of the group and the standard deviation, you can successfully predict someone's percentile rank in the group.

Confused? Let me give you an example. If instead of 5 people's heights, we had 100 people, we could figure out their rank in height JUST by knowing the average, standard deviation, and their height. We wouldn't need to know each person's height and manually rank them, we could just predict their rank based on three numbers.

What this means is that you can take your PERCENTILE rank that is often given with your test and relate this to your RELATIVE IQ of people taking the test - that is, your IQ relative to the people taking the test. Obviously, there's no way to know your actual IQ because the people taking a standardized test are usually not very good samples of the general population- many of those with extremely low IQ's never achieve a level of success or competency necessary to complete a typical standardized test. In fact, professional psychologists who measure IQ actually have to use non-written tests that can fairly measure the IQ of those not able to complete a traditional test.

The bottom line is to not take your test score too seriously, but it is fun to compute your "relative IQ" among the people who took the test with you. I've done the calculations below. Just look up your percentile rank in the left and then you'll see your "relative IQ" for your test in the right hand column-

Percentile Rank	Your Relative IQ		Percentile Rank	Your Relative IQ
99	135		59	103
98	131		58	103
97	128		57	103
96	126		56	102
95	125		55	102
94	123		54	102
93	122		53	101
92	121		52	101
91	120		51	100
90	119		50	100
89	118		49	100
88	118		48	99
87	117		47	99
86	116		46	98
85	116		45	98
84	115		44	98
83	114		43	97
82	114		42	97
81	113		41	97
80	113		40	96
79	112		39	96
78	112		38	95
77	111		37	95
76	111		36	95
75	110		35	94
74	110		34	94
73	109		33	93
72	109		32	93
71	108		31	93
70	108		30	92
69	107		29	92
68	107		28	91
67	107		27	91
66	106		26	90
65	106		25	90
64	105		24	89
63	105		23	89
62	105		22	88
61	104		21	88
60	104		20	87

Special Report: What is Test Anxiety and How to Overcome It?

The very nature of tests caters to some level of anxiety, nervousness or tension, just as we feel for any important event that occurs in our lives. A little bit of anxiety or nervousness can be a good thing. It helps us with motivation, and makes achievement just that much sweeter. However, too much anxiety can be a problem; especially if it hinders our ability to function and perform.

"Test anxiety," is the term that refers to the emotional reactions that some test-takers experience when faced with a test or exam. Having a fear of testing and exams is based upon a rational fear, since the test-taker's performance can shape the course of an academic career. Nevertheless, experiencing excessive fear of examinations will only interfere with the test-takers ability to perform and his/her chances to be successful.

There are a large variety of causes that can contribute to the development and sensation of test anxiety. These include, but are not limited to lack of performance and worrying about issues surrounding the test.

Lack of Preparation

Lack of preparation can be identified by the following behaviors or situations:

Not scheduling enough time to study, and therefore cramming the night before the test or exam
Managing time poorly, to create the sensation that there is not enough time to do everything
Failing to organize the text information in advance, so that the study material consists of the entire text and not simply the pertinent information
Poor overall studying habits

Worrying, on the other hand, can be related to both the test taker, and many other factors around him/her that will be affected by the results of the test. These include worrying about:

Previous performances on similar exams, or exams in general
How friends and other students are achieving
The negative consequences that will result from a poor grade or failure

There are three primary elements to test anxiety: 1) Physical components, which involve the same typical bodily reactions as those to acute anxiety (to be discussed below), 2) Emotional factors have to do with fear or panic, and. 3) Mental or cognitive issues concerning attention spans and memory abilities.

Physical Signals

There are many different symptoms of test anxiety, and these are not limited to mental and emotional strain. Frequently there are a range of physical signals that will let a test taker know that he/she is suffering from test anxiety. These bodily changes can include the following:
Perspiring
Sweaty palms
Wet, trembling hands
Nausea
Dry mouth
A knot in the stomach
Headache
Faintness
Muscle tension
Aching shoulders, back and neck
Rapid heart beat
Feeling too hot/cold

To recognize the sensation of test anxiety, a test-taker should monitor himself/herself for the following sensations:
- The physical distress symptoms as listed above
- Emotional sensitivity, expressing emotional feelings such as the need to cry or laugh too much, or a sensation of anger or helplessness
- A decreased ability to think, causing the test-taker to blank out or have racing thoughts that are hard to organize or control.

Though most students will feel some level of anxiety when faced with a test or exam, the majority can cope with that anxiety and maintain it at a manageable level. However, those who cannot are faced with a very real and very serious condition, which can and should be controlled for the immeasurable benefit of this sufferer.

Naturally, these sensations lead to negative results for the testing experience. The most common effects of test anxiety have to do with nervousness and mental blocking.

Nervousness

Nervousness can appear in several different levels:
- The test-taker's difficulty, or even inability, to read and understand the questions on the test
- The difficulty or inability to organize thoughts to a coherent form
- The difficulty or inability to recall key words and concepts relating to the testing questions (especially essays)
- The receipt of poor grades on a test, though the test material was well known by the test taker

Conversely, a person may also experience mental blocking, which involves:
- Blanking out on test questions

- Only remembering the correct answers to the questions when the test has already finished.

Fortunately for test anxiety sufferers, beating these feelings, to a large degree, has to do with proper preparation. When a test taker has a feeling of preparedness, then anxiety will be dramatically lessened.

The first step to resolving anxiety issues is to distinguish which of the two types of anxiety are being suffered. If the anxiety is a direct result of a lack of preparation, this should be considered a normal reaction, and the anxiety level (as opposed to the test results) shouldn't be anything to worry about. However, if, when adequately prepared, the test-taker still panics, blanks out, or seems to overreact, this is not a fully rational reaction. While this can be considered normal too, there are many ways to combat and overcome these effects.

Remember that anxiety cannot be entirely eliminated; however, there are ways to minimize it, to make the anxiety easier to manage. Preparation is one of the best ways to minimize test anxiety. Therefore the following techniques are wise in order to best fight off any anxiety that may want to build.

To begin with, try to avoid cramming before a test, whenever it is possible. By trying to memorize an entire term's worth of information in one day, you'll be shocking your system, and not giving yourself a very good chance to absorb the information. This is an easy path to anxiety, so for those who suffer from test anxiety, cramming should not even be considered an option.

Instead of cramming, work throughout the semester to combine all of the material which is presented throughout the semester, and work on it gradually as the course goes by, making sure to master the main concepts first, leaving minor details for a week or so before the test.

To study for the upcoming exam, be sure to pose questions that may be on the examination, to gauge the ability to answer them by integrating the ideas from your texts, notes and lectures, as well as any supplementary readings.

If it is truly impossible to cover all of the information that was covered in that particular term, concentrate on the most important portions, that can be covered very well. Learn these concepts as best as possible, so that when the test comes, a goal can be made to use these concepts as presentations of your knowledge.

In addition to study habits, changes in attitude are critical to beating a struggle with test anxiety. In fact, an improvement of the perspective over the entire test-taking experience can actually help a test taker to enjoy studying and therefore improve the overall experience. Be certain not to overemphasize the significance of the grade - know that the result of the test is neither a reflection of self worth, nor is it a measure of intelligence; one grade will not predict a person's future success.

To improve an overall testing outlook, the following steps should be tried:
1. Keeping in mind that the most reasonable expectation for taking a test is to expect to try to demonstrate as much of what you know as you possibly can.

2. Reminding ourselves that a test is only one test; this is not the only one, and there will be others.
3. The thought of thinking of oneself in an irrational, all-or-nothing term should be avoided at all costs.
4. A reward should be designated for after the test, so there's something to look forward to. Whether it be going to a movie, going out to eat, or simply visiting friends, schedule it in advance, and do it no matter what result is expected on the exam.

Test-takers should also keep in mind that the basics are some of the most important things, even beyond anti-anxiety techniques and studying. Never neglect the basic social, emotional and biological needs, in order to try to absorb information. In order to best achieve, these three factors must be held as just as important as the studying itself.

Study Steps

Remember the following important steps for studying:

Maintain healthy nutrition and exercise habits. Continue both your recreational activities and social pass times. These both contribute to your physical and emotional well being.

Be certain to get a good amount of sleep, especially the night before the test, because when you're overtired you are not able to perform to the best of your best ability.

Keep the studying pace to a moderate level by taking breaks when they are needed, and varying the work whenever possible, to keep the mind fresh instead of getting bored.

When enough studying has been done that all the material that can be learned has been learned, and the test taker is prepared for the test, stop studying and do something relaxing such as listening to music, watching a movie, or taking a warm bubble bath.

There are also many other techniques to minimize the uneasiness or apprehension that is experienced along with test anxiety before, during, or even after the examination. In fact, there are a great deal of things that can be done to stop anxiety from interfering with lifestyle and performance. Again, remember that anxiety will not be eliminated entirely, and it shouldn't be. Otherwise that "up" feeling for exams would not exist, and most of us depend on that sensation to perform better than usual. However, this anxiety has to be at a level that is manageable.

Of course, as we have just discussed, being prepared for the exam is half the battle right away. Attending all classes, finding out what knowledge will be expected on the exam, and knowing the exam schedules are easy steps to lowering anxiety.

Keeping up with work will remove the need to cram, and efficient study habits will eliminate wasted time.

Studying should be done in an ideal location for concentration, so that it is simple to become interested in the material and give it complete attention.

A method such as SQ3R (Survey, Question, Read, Recite, Review) is a wonderful key to follow to make sure that the study habits are as effective as possible, especially in the case of learning from a textbook. Flashcards are great techniques for memorization.

Learning to take good notes will mean that notes will be full of useful information, so that less sifting will need to be done to seek out what is pertinent for studying. Reviewing notes after class and then again on occasion will keep the information fresh in the mind. From notes that have been taken summary sheets and outlines can be made for simpler reviewing.

A study group can also be a very motivational and helpful place to study, as there will be a sharing of ideas, all of the minds can work together, to make sure that everyone understands, and the studying will be made more interesting because it will be a social occasion.

Basically, though, as long as the test-taker remains organized and self confident, with efficient study habits, less time will need to be spent studying, and higher grades will be achieved.

To become self-confident, there are many useful steps. The first of these is "self talk." It has been shown through extensive research, that self-talk for students who suffer from test anxiety, should be well monitored, in order to make sure that it contributes to self confidence as opposed to sinking the student. Frequently the self talk of test-anxious students is negative or self-defeating, thinking that everyone else is smarter and faster, that they always mess up, and that if they don't do well, they'll fail the entire course. It is important to decreasing anxiety that awareness is made of self talk. Try writing any negative self thoughts and then disputing them with a positive statement instead. Begin self-encouragement as though it was a friend speaking. Repeat positive statements to help reprogram the mind to believing in successes instead of failures.

Helpful Techniques

Other extremely helpful techniques include:

- Self-visualization of doing well and reaching goals
- While aiming for an "A" level of understanding, don't try to "overprotect" by setting your expectations lower. This will only convince the mind to stop studying in order to meet the lower expectations.
- Don't make comparisons with the results or habits of other students. These are individual factors, and different things work for different people, causing different results.
- Strive to become an expert in learning what works well, and what can be done in order to improve. Consider collecting this data in a journal.
- Create rewards for after studying instead of doing things before studying that will only turn into avoidance behaviors.
- Make a practice of relaxing - by using methods such as progressive relaxation, self-hypnosis, guided imagery, etc - in order to make relaxation an automatic sensation.

- Work on creating a state of relaxed concentration so that concentrating will take on the focus of the mind, so that none will be wasted on worrying.
- Take good care of the physical self by eating well and getting enough sleep.
- Plan time for exercise and stick to this plan.

Beyond these techniques, there are other methods to be used before, during and after the test that will help the test-taker perform well in addition to overcoming anxiety.

Before the exam comes the academic preparation. This involves establishing a study schedule and beginning at least one week before the actual date of the test. By doing this, the anxiety of not having enough time to study for the test will automatically be eliminated. Moreover, this will make the studying a much more effective experience, ensuring that the learning will be an easier process. This relieves much undue pressure on the test-taker.

Summary sheets, note cards, and flash cards with the main concepts and examples of these main concepts should be prepared in advance of the actual studying time. A topic should never be eliminated from this process. By omitting a topic because it isn't expected to be on the test is only setting up the test-taker for anxiety should it actually appear on the exam. Utilize the course syllabus for laying out the topics that should be studied. Carefully go over the notes that were made in class, paying special attention to any of the issues that the professor took special care to emphasize while lecturing in class. In the textbooks, use the chapter review, or if possible, the chapter tests, to begin your review.

It may even be possible to ask the instructor what information will be covered on the exam, or what the format of the exam will be (for example, multiple choice, essay, free form, true-false). Additionally, see if it is possible to find out how many questions will be on the test. If a review sheet or sample test has been offered by the professor, make good use of it, above anything else, for the preparation for the test. Another great resource for getting to know the examination is reviewing tests from previous semesters. Use these tests to review, and aim to achieve a 100% score on each of the possible topics. With a few exceptions, the goal that you set for yourself is the highest one that you will reach.

Take all of the questions that were assigned as homework, and rework them to any other possible course material. The more problems reworked, the more skill and confidence will form as a result. When forming the solution to a problem, write out each of the steps. Don't simply do head work. By doing as many steps on paper as possible, much clarification and therefore confidence will be formed. Do this with as many homework problems as possible, before checking the answers. By checking the answer after each problem, reinforcement will exist, that will not be on the exam. Study situations should be as exam-like as possible, to prime the test-taker's system for the experience. By waiting to check the answers at the end, a psychological advantage will be formed, to decrease the stress factor.

Another fantastic reason for not cramming is the avoidance of confusion in concepts, especially when it comes to mathematics. 8-10 hours of study will become one hundred percent more effective if it is spread out over a week or at least several days, instead of doing it all in one sitting. Recognize that the human brain requires time in order to assimilate new material, so frequent breaks and a span of study time over several days will be much more beneficial.

Additionally, don't study right up until the point of the exam. Studying should stop a minimum of one hour before the exam begins. This allows the brain to rest and put things in their proper order. This will also provide the time to become as relaxed as possible when going into the examination room. The test-taker will also have time to eat well and eat sensibly. Know that the brain needs food as much as the rest of the body. With enough food and enough sleep, as well as a relaxed attitude, the body and the mind are primed for success.

Avoid any anxious classmates who are talking about the exam. These students only spread anxiety, and are not worth sharing the anxious sentimentalities.

Before the test also involves creating a positive attitude, so mental preparation should also be a point of concentration. There are many keys to creating a positive attitude. Should fears become rushing in, make a visualization of taking the exam, doing well, and seeing an A written on the paper. Write out a list of affirmations that will bring a feeling of confidence, such as "I am doing well in my English class," "I studied well and know my material," "I enjoy this class." Even if the affirmations aren't believed at first, it sends a positive message to the subconscious which will result in an alteration of the overall belief system, which is the system that creates reality.

If a sensation of panic begins, work with the fear and imagine the very worst! Work through the entire scenario of not passing the test, failing the entire course, and dropping out of school, followed by not getting a job, and pushing a shopping cart through the dark alley where you'll live. This will place things into perspective! Then, practice deep breathing and create a visualization of the opposite situation - achieving an "A" on the exam, passing the entire course, receiving the degree at a graduation ceremony.

On the day of the test, there are many things to be done to ensure the best results, as well as the calmest outlook. The following stages are suggested in order to maximize test-taking potential:
Begin the examination day with a moderate breakfast, and avoid any coffee or beverages with caffeine if the test taker is prone to jitters. Even people who are used to managing caffeine can feel jittery or light-headed when it is taken on a test day.

Attempt to do something that is relaxing before the examination begins. As last minute cramming clouds the mastering of overall concepts, it is better to use this time to create a calming outlook.

Be certain to arrive at the test location well in advance, in order to provide time to select a location that is away from doors, windows and other distractions, as well as giving enough time to relax before the test begins.

Keep away from anxiety generating classmates who will upset the sensation of stability and relaxation that is being attempted before the exam.

Should the waiting period before the exam begins cause anxiety, create a self-distraction by reading a light magazine or something else that is relaxing and simple.

During the exam itself, read the entire exam from beginning to end, and find out how much time should be allotted to each individual problem. Once writing the exam, should more time be taken for a problem, it should be abandoned, in order to begin another problem. If there is time at the end, the unfinished problem can always be returned to and completed.

Read the instructions very carefully - twice - so that unpleasant surprises won't follow during or after the exam has ended.

When writing the exam, pretend that the situation is actually simply the completion of homework within a library, or at home. This will assist in forming a relaxed atmosphere, and will allow the brain extra focus for the complex thinking function.

Begin the exam with all of the questions with which the most confidence is felt. This will build the confidence level regarding the entire exam and will begin a quality momentum. This will also create encouragement for trying the problems where uncertainty resides.

Going with the "gut instinct" is always the way to go when solving a problem. Second guessing should be avoided at all costs. Have confidence in the ability to do well.

For essay questions, create an outline in advance that will keep the mind organized and make certain that all of the points are remembered. For multiple choice, read every answer, even if the correct one has been spotted - a better one may exist.

Continue at a pace that is reasonable and not rushed, in order to be able to work carefully. Provide enough time to go over the answers at the end, to check for small errors that can be corrected.

Should a feeling of panic begin, breathe deeply, and think of the feeling of the body releasing sand through its pores. Visualize a calm, peaceful place, and include all of the sights, sounds and sensations of this image. Continue the deep breathing, and take a few minutes to continue this with closed eyes. When all is well again, return to the test. If a "blanking" occurs for a certain question, skip it and move on to the next question. There will be time to return to the other question later. Get everything done that can be done, first, to guarantee all the grades that can be compiled, and to build all of the confidence possible. Then return to the weaker questions to build the marks from there.

Remember, one's own reality can be created, so as long as the belief is there, success will follow. And remember: anxiety can happen later, right now, there's an exam to be written!

After the examination is complete, whether there is a feeling for a good grade or a bad grade, don't dwell on the exam, and be certain to follow through on the reward that was promised...and enjoy it! Don't dwell on any mistakes that have been made, as there is nothing that can be done at this point anyway.

Additionally, don't begin to study for the next test right away. Do something relaxing for a while, and let the mind relax and prepare itself to begin absorbing information again.

From the results of the exam - both the grade and the entire experience, be certain to learn from what has gone on. Perfect studying habits and work some more on confidence in order to make the next examination experience even better than the last one.

Learn to avoid places where openings occurred for laziness, procrastination and day dreaming.

Use the time between this exam and the next one to learn to relax better (even learning to relax on cue), so that any anxiety can be controlled during the next exam. Learn how to relax the body. Slouch in your chair if that helps. Tighten and then relax all of the different muscle groups, one group at a time, beginning with the feet and then working all the way up to the neck and face. This will ultimately relax the muscles more than they were to begin with. Learn how to breathe deeply and comfortably, and focus on this breathing going in and out as a relaxing thought. With every exhale, repeat the word "relax."

As common as test anxiety is, it is very possible to overcome it. Make yourself one of the test-takers who overcome this frustrating hindrance.

Special Report: Retaking the Test: What Are Your Chances at Improving Your Score?

After going through the experience of taking a major test, many test takers feel that once is enough. The test usually comes during a period of transition in the test taker's life, and taking the test is only one of a series of important events. With so many distractions and conflicting recommendations, it may be difficult for a test taker to rationally determine whether or not he should retake the test after viewing his scores.

The importance of the test usually only adds to the burden of the retake decision. However, don't be swayed by emotion. There a few simple questions that you can ask yourself to guide you as you try to determine whether a retake would improve your score:

1. What went wrong? Why wasn't your score what you expected?

Can you point to a single factor or problem that you feel caused the low score? Were you sick on test day? Was there an emotional upheaval in your life that caused a distraction? Were you late for the test or not able to use the full time allotment? If you can point to any of these specific, individual problems, then a retake should definitely be considered.

2. Is there enough time to improve?

Many problems that may show up in your score report may take a lot of time for improvement. A deficiency in a particular math skill may require weeks or months of tutoring and studying to improve. If you have enough time to improve an identified weakness, then a retake should definitely be considered.

3. How will additional scores be used? Will a score average, highest score, or most recent score be used?

Different test scores may be handled completely differently. If you've taken the test multiple times, sometimes your highest score is used, sometimes your average score is computed and used, and sometimes your most recent score is used. Make sure you understand what method will be used to evaluate your scores, and use that to help you determine whether a retake should be considered.

4. Are my practice tests scores significantly higher than my actual test score?

If you have taken a lot of practice tests and are consistently scoring at a much higher level than your actual test score, then you should consider a retake. However, if you've taken five practice tests and only one of your scores was higher than your actual test score, or if your practice tests scores was only slightly higher than your actual test score, then it is unlikely that you will significantly increase your score.

5. Do I need perfect scores or will I be able to live with this score? Will this score still allow me to follow my dreams?

What kind of score is acceptable to you? Is your current score "good enough?" Do you have to have a certain score in order to pursue the future of your dreams? If you won't be happy with your current score, and there's no way that you could live with it, then you should consider a retake. However, don't get your hopes up. If you are looking for significant improvement, that may or may not be possible. But if you won't be happy otherwise, it is at least worth the effort.

Remember that there are other considerations. To achieve your dream, it is likely that your grades may also be taken into account. A great test score is usually not the only thing necessary to succeed. Make sure that you aren't overemphasizing the importance of a high test score.

Furthermore, a retake does not always result in a higher score. Some test takers will score lower on a retake, rather than higher. One study shows that one-fourth of test takers will achieve a significant improvement in test score, while one-sixth of test takers will actually show a decrease. While this shows that most test takers will improve, the majority will only improve their scores a little and a retake may not be worth the test taker's effort.

Finally, if a test is taken only once and is considered in the added context of good grades on the part of a test taker, the person reviewing the grades and scores may be tempted to assume that the test taker just had a bad day while taking the test, and may discount the low test score in favor of the high grades. But if the test is retaken and the scores are approximately the same, then the validity of the low scores are only confirmed. Therefore, a retake could actually hurt a test taker by definitely bracketing a test taker's score ability to a limited range.

Special Report: Additional Bonus Material

Due to our efforts to try to keep this book to a manageable length, we've created a link that will give you access to all of your additional bonus material.

Please visit http://www.mometrix.com/bonus948/priisplangpath to access the information.